Computer Science
Pure and Simple

Book 1

for Homeschoolers

by Phyllis Wheeler, Don Sleeth, Virginia Sparks & Laura Breidenbach

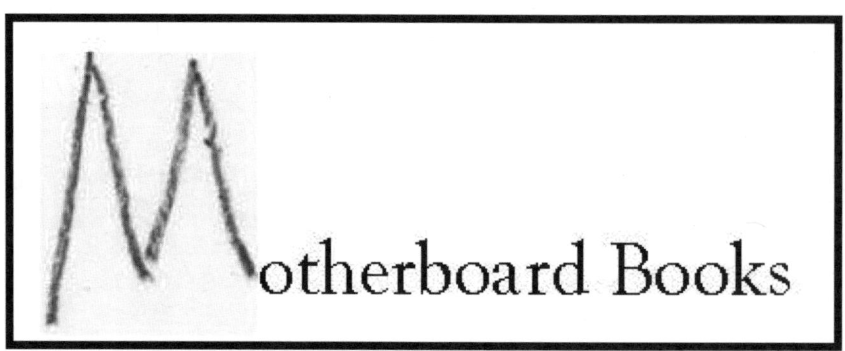

ISBN 0-9749653-0-8

Motherboard Books

PO Box 430041

St. Louis, MO 63143

www.motherboardbooks.com

About the Authors:

Phyllis Wheeler teaches a computer science class to a homeschool co-op in St. Louis. She included and adapted material written by several people in the class work, and has written it all down for this book. Now a homeschooling mother, she has worked in the aerospace industry as a mechanical engineer. Along the way she has written some computer programs and taken some computer courses. She has also worked as a newspaper reporter and free-lance writer. She has bachelor's degrees in English from Smith College and in mechanical engineering from Washington University in St. Louis.

Don Sleeth is a computer professional in Canada who wrote a manuscript of lessons to teach his daughter programming with MicroWorlds Logo.

Virginia Sparks has worked in computer science as software developer and desktop publisher and is currently a homeschooling mother. She has a B.A. in Math and Computer Science from Blackburn College, Carlinville, Illinois.

Laura Breidenbach is a professional Web site developer who guided our students through creating a Web site using Cool Page.

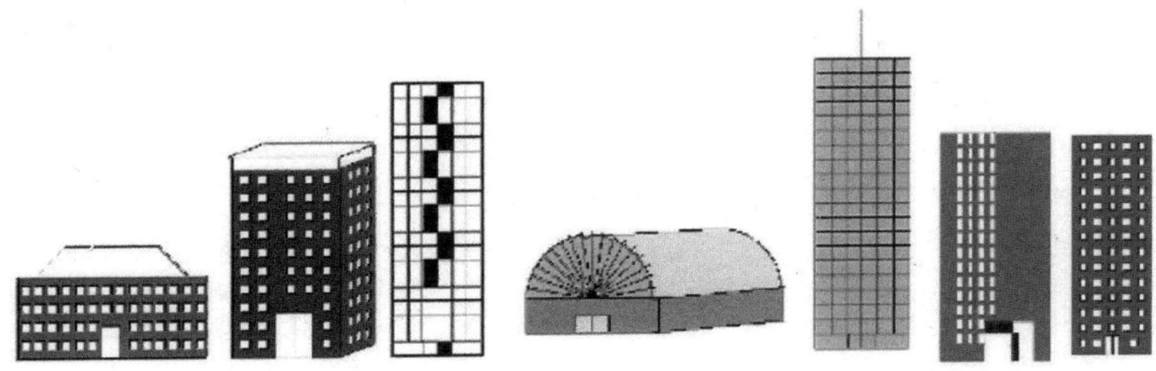

These are the buildings our senior high students created using Logo commands.

Acknowledgments

In many ways our homeschool co-op computer class and the book that resulted have been a collaborative effort. I would like to acknowledge the contribution of:

- John A. Sparks, also known as Gio, who made all this possible through generous donations of his time to set up and maintain our homeschool computer lab
- Steven Sittser, who donated his time to provide computer lab time for the students in the evening.
- Clayton Community Church, which has gone out of its way to support the co-op and the computer lab.

Phyllis Wheeler

Table of Contents

Introduction

Computers are all around us, and the workplace clearly requires them. Many public schools use computers in the classrooms. In fact, eleven states require a computer course for high-school graduation.[1] Many of the best jobs that will be open for our kids when they grow up will involve programming. And so homeschoolers really need to be learning computer science.

The earlier kids start a complex subject, the better. But many home-schooling parents think they are not qualified to teach computers. In the meantime, their kids may be falling behind in acquiring a skill that they will surely need.

If you need some help teaching computer skills to your kids, this book is for you. It provides a broad introduction to basic computer science and usage, for you and your kids! You CAN give your kids the early training in computers that will make them comfortable in this medium all their lives.

This book grew out of the efforts of a homeschool co-op in St. Louis, Missouri. It represents a transcription of our efforts to teach a variety of basic computer skills to computer novices, 5th grade through high school, during the course of a year, with adjustments made for what worked well and what didn't. So the curriculum has been tested, you might say.

Book structure

We provide a mixture of lessons. We included use of common office applications, such as word processors and spread sheets, along with basic programming (using MicroWorlds Logo) and Web site design. (We strongly recommend that the student also learn typing using a fun computer application such as Jump Start Typing, Typing Tutor, or Mavis Beacon Teaches Typing.)

The book is organized in an unusual way. Instead of the typical textbook organization, with big chapters on each topic (word processing, spread sheets, Web sites, and programming), we have provided a mixture of lessons on various topics at a beginning level. Then we move to more advanced levels on the various topics. This is intended to mimic the way we most easily learn a new skill—a little of this, a little of that, some repetition, and again more of this and more of that.

The suggested pacing for this material is one lesson per week, allowing time for exercises and practice before moving on. But for the Web site construction lessons, much more time is required—five to six weeks each. Our homeschool co-op, meeting weekly, took one school year to get through these 21 lessons.

Troubleshooting: For the homeschool teacher, computer expertise is not required, although some experience with computers is desirable. We provide an answer key in the back of the book. We suggest that you let your student puzzle over a problem for a while before handing out some hints and then finally if necessary letting him see the answer. For troubleshooting programs that don't work, look for suggestions in the text and at the troubleshooting guides for HTML and MicroWorlds in the Appendix.

---

[1] National Center for Educational Statistics, http://nces.ed.gov/pubs2003/digest02/tables/dt152.asp

Why choose MicroWorlds?

This book teaches programming using MicroWorlds, an application based on the Logo computer language. It does our job admirably:

- Using graphics, it instantly shows young programmers the results of their efforts. It makes computer science fun instead of difficult.
- It introduces students to the universal elements of computer languages, including variables and logic. Once students learn one computer language, it will be easy to pick up another.
- MicroWorlds 2.0 will work on older computers as well as newer ones.
- Visual Basic provides a similar result and is used in the workplace. But the Microsoft application is more complex to learn and costs the user $109 per computer as of fall, 2003.
- MicroWorlds' parent company, LCSI, has provided us licensing to sell the software for single home use for considerably less than the cost of Visual Basic.
- There are inexpensive or free computer applications out there, but they don't provide the programming result in a graphic form. We feel this graphic result is vital to grab and keep kids' interest.

Minimum Computer Requirements

This course was designed with a PC in mind, running Microsoft Word, Microsoft Excel, a browser (Internet Explorer or Netscape) and MicroWorlds. We also suggest a free download of a PC Web page editor called Cool Page. If you have a MacIntosh with Microsoft Word and Excel installed, you should be able to follow the book except for Cool Page. MicroWorlds will install on a MacIntosh.

Here are **MicroWorlds 2.0** requirements:

Mac: Operating System 7.0 & higher
16 MB RAM
CD-ROM drive
PC: Windows 95/98/NT/Me/2000/XP Operating System
486DX processor (66 MHz or better recommended) or Pentium
16 MB RAM
CD-ROM drive

Here are **MicroWorlds EX** requirements:

Mac: Under development at printing time
PC: Windows 98/NT/Me/2000/XP Operating System
Pentium processor or higher
32 MB RAM
CD ROM drive
Support for 32 bit color mode
Sound card

#1 Word Processing

My job is to show you how to use your word processor as a tool to create high-quality documents. Word processing is easy and fun, and it is a good place to start.

Getting started

Run your word processor by double-clicking on its icon. (We are using Microsoft Word, but others will be similar.)

What you see is called your desktop. Along the top is a list of pull-down menus: **File, Edit, View,** and so on. Below that is a row of icons called a toolbar.

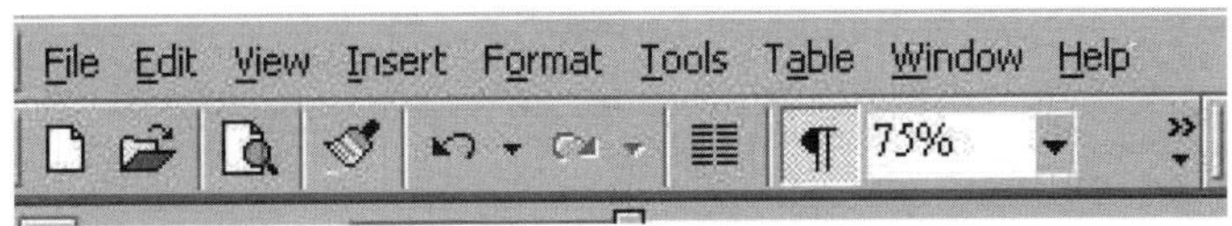

The page that pops up for you to type on is called the default page. It has settings that you can use for most of your projects.

Let's type a bit of text and then select it by clicking the mouse button down near it, passing the arrow over it, and then letting the button go. It should be highlighted in black.

Let's change the font, the way the print looks. There are two ways to do that—with a menu, and with the toolbar. Guess what menu would you look under to change the font? Try some by letting your mouse arrow pause over the menu name.

You'll find font under the **Format** menu.

Now from the toolbar, how can we change the font? Find the icon that lists a font name, such as Times New Roman, with a down arrow next to it. Click on the down arrow to see a list, and select a different one. You'll see the font change in the words you selected.

In the toolbar, there is an icon for the printer, and so on. Let your mouse arrow pause for a moment over an icon, and it will tell you what it does.

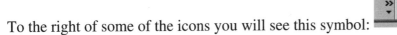

To the right of some of the icons you will see this symbol: 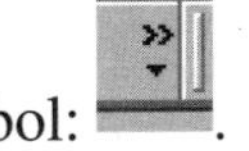.

If you click on it, you will see more icons. There are too many to be displayed at the same time. The ones displayed are the ones you have used recently.

You can also do tasks using keyboard shortcuts. You can print your page by going to the **File** menu and then **print**. But you can do the same by striking the **control** key and the **p** key at the same time. Or you can save under the same name by going to the **File** menu, then clicking **save.** Or you can do the same by striking **control** and **s**. If you are wondering what the shortcuts are, find the command in a pull-down menu, and it will also tell you the keyboard shortcut. When you get used to the keyboard shortcuts, they are faster than using the menus.

Type a title, "This is my page," and push enter. Then type another line with the date, push enter, and another line with your name.

Save your file. From the File menu, click on "save as."

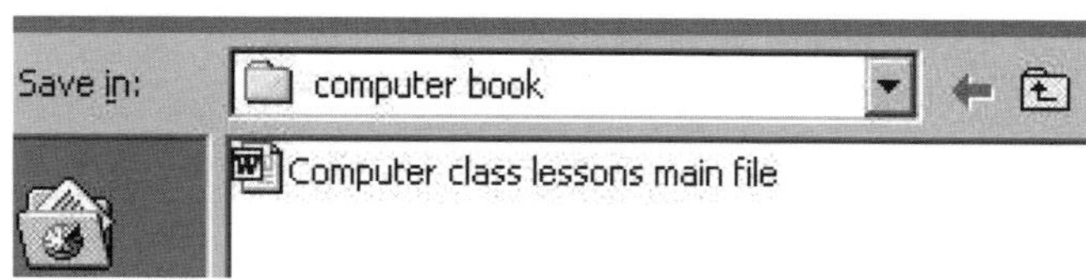

There is a file name listed at the top of the window with a down-arrow (a triangle). If you click the down arrow, it will show lots of other folders. If you click the yellow folder with the up-arrow, you'll go up a folder level. Experiment and see if you can put your file in "my documents." This is in the main folder of your hard drive, C:. Near the bottom of the window, there's a blank space for you to type a name. Or maybe the software has already input the first line of your file as the name. Choose a name and click on "save." Be sure you remember *where* you saved it!

Now let's select some more text. Remember how? Select your title by using the mouse—press the left mouse button when you get to one side of the word, "paint" it across the word, and pick it up when you get to the other side of the word. The selected text now has a black background.

Let's change the text alignment. We want our title to be centered, not on the left side where it starts out. Find icons in the toolbar that look like six lines arranged slightly differently.

When the mouse arrow pauses over them, they say "Align left," "Align center," and "Align right." With text selected, choose Align center. Your title hops over to the center of the page.

(If your word processor doesn't have these icons, do this: select the text. Go to the **Format** menu, then **Paragraph**, then **Align**. Choose **Align center**.)

If your word processor wants to line up everything, including what you have NOT highlighted, then push the undo button to undo the extra. The undo button looks like this:

Do the same with the date, only choose Align right. Leave your name aligned to the left where it was to begin with.

Let's change the font size. Select the title again. In the toolbar, find the words "Times New Roman." That's the name of the font. Next to it is a 12. That is the size of the font, in "points."

Click on the arrow next to the 12 to see a list of other sizes. Click on one. Any text you have selected (highlighted in black) will change size to this size now. Now, select the date and make it smaller. (You can also change the color of your selected text when you use the **Format** menu and select **Font** from there.)

Let's make some corrections. To select a word, double click on a spot in a word. (To select the paragraph, triple click.) Once you have selected a word, you can retype over that word very easily—just start typing, and the original selection disappears. Your newly typed word takes its place.

Did you make a mistake? Find the "undo" icon. There is no need to select anything first. Click the icon once to undo the last change you made. Click it twice to undo the last two, and so on.

From the **File** pull-down menu, click on **Page setup**. Look for places to change the orientation of the

page from **landscape** (horizontal) to **portrait** (vertical).

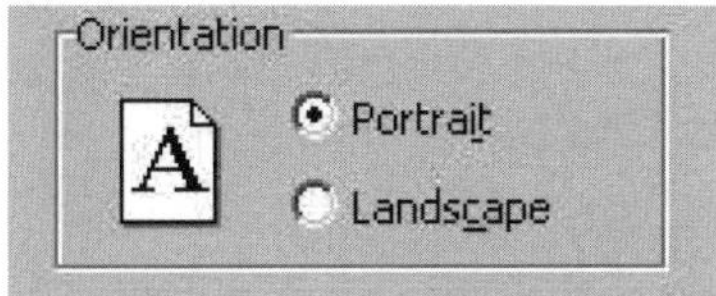

Click on **landscape**. What happens? (Some printers may require you to change the printer setup to landscape before printing. To do this, from the Start menu find the control panel, and then the printers.)

Let's move some text. Double click on a few words to select them. A mouse arrow appears. Point the arrow to the text, and push down on the left mouse button. Hold it down, and "drag" the highlighted text to another place on the page. When you let go, the words move to the new spot.

There's another way to do this: copy and paste. You can move words around on a page, too. But with this method, you can actually take text from your word processor and paste it into another application, such as your email, your spreadsheet, or your drawing program. This is because the computer copies the text onto a "clipboard" that all other applications can see too. To use this, select some text, go to the **Edit** menu, and select **copy**. This invisibly puts the text on the clipboard. Now, move your cursor somewhere else (even in another application), go to **Edit**, and select **paste**. It puts a copy of what's on the clipboard in that spot. (Keyboard shortcut for **copy** is **control-c**, and for **paste** is **control-v**.)

Let's make our text **bold**, *italic (slanted)*, or underlined. Select a word, and then click on the letter in the toolbar: **B** for bold, ***I*** for italic, and **U** for underline.

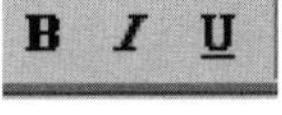

Now, let's insert a text table. From the pull-down Table menu, select Insert, then Table. Choose one with five rows and two columns. Click OK. What do you get? A table you can fill with whatever you like – schedules, science project data, and so on. Try putting text in the boxes. Make another table with fewer rows and more columns.

The finishing touches

Do you want to run a final spell check on the file? Go to the **Tools** menu and select **spelling and grammar.** The spell-checker pops up. Want to check spelling on a single word or paragraph? Select the word or paragraph first, and then click on the spell checker.

Now you want to save your file. You already gave it a name and put it in a folder. To save the latest version under that same name, you need to go to the **File** menu and click on **save**. Or, you can use the keyboard shortcut **control-s**. Your word processor gives the file name an extension, such as ".doc," that allows the computer to know how to open it later.

There are several ways to print your file:

- From the **File** menu, click on **print**. The printer page appears. For one copy, press enter.
- From your keyboard, press **control-p**. The printer page appears.
- From the **File** menu, click on **print preview**. It will show you what your work looks like. From there you can click on **print**. A page appears asking you for details on numbers of copies and so on. To get one copy, press enter.

Close your file by clicking on the File menu, then "close."

Some other good things to know

To retrieve your file, open the word processor, go to the **File** menu, and click on **open**. Select a file to open. You may need to remember what folder it is in, and what folder that is in.

If you get stuck, use the help system. Here is how: click on the **Help** menu. Click on the word **Help** just above the toolbar. Follow directions to search for help under a keyword.

#2 Logo Procedures & Input

What will I learn?

These Logo lessons are intended to teach individual students in grades 5-12 the basics of computer use and programming. We will teach you some basic computer skills. We will also teach you how and why to write programs that will work properly and can be improved on as time goes by. This will give you a solid foundation in programming techniques so you can develop programs in any language.

What computer language?

There are many different programming languages, just like there are many languages spoken in the world. Human languages all have verbs, nouns and adjectives. Programming languages too have similar elements, like procedures and variables. It is these building blocks that are basic to computer programming in any language that it is important to learn. Once you learn one computer language, it is much easier to learn the next and the next.

Even though it is not the computer language that is important, I still had to choose one to use. I wanted a language that would allow you the student, to build programs that were fun and complete, in a fairly short time. There is a language that is written specifically to teach computer-programming concepts to young people, and that language is Logo. So I chose Logo.

Just like human languages can be spoken with different accents, so it is with computer languages. The 'version' of Logo that I use in these lessons is from a commercial product named "MicroWorlds" from Logo Computer Systems Inc.

Where are we headed?

We will learn techniques that will allow you to draw your own interesting scenes and add lots of movement and animation.

What is a program?

A program is *a list of instructions to the computer*. Let's suppose we are going to give someone a list of simple instructions in English on how to set the table. This list of instructions might look like this:

get a plate from the cupboard
walk to the table
put it on the table
return to the cupboard
get a glass
... and so on.

But a set of instructions for a computer is written using a specific list of words that the computer can understand. For example, forward 50 means go forward 50 turtle paces. These action words for the computer are *procedures*.

What's a turtle, you ask? It's our little drawing partner on the screen. We pretend that it is carrying a pen that it can put down, to draw, and pick up, to move around without drawing. It can wear various suits of clothes—it can look like a horse, a dog, even a house or a pond. The nice thing about it is that it obeys our every command, so long as we use words it can understand.

So, if a program is a list of instructions to the computer and an instruction is a list of procedures and MicroWorlds already knows piles of procedures, we must be ready to write a program!

Instructions and Procedures

We need to begin by locating our turtle. In MicroWorlds 2.0, this is no problem; there it is, when we open the program. With MicroWorlds EX, we have to hatch a turtle by clicking on the icon at the top which looks vaguely like a green turtle emerging from an egg. Then click on the screen, and you have a turtle.

Now, let's start with an instruction.

In *the Command Center* (the gray area at the bottom of the screen) type **cc** (stands for clear the Command Center) and press **Enter** to execute the command. Then write the following line:

pd forward 50 right 90 forward 50 right 90 forward 50 right 90 forward 50 right 90

When the cursor is at the very end, press **Enter**. Presto! Our first instruction causes the turtle to draw a square.

Let's analyze our one long line of instruction. All the words you see on the line are names of procedures:

pd: a procedure that puts the current turtle's pen down and requires no inputs and has no outputs

forward: a procedure that moves the current turtle in the direction its head is pointing by a certain number of steps. The number is a required input.

right: a procedure that turns the current turtle to the right by a number of degrees. The number is a required input.

The last two procedures require a number as their input. One very important thing to notice is that some procedures require inputs and some don't.

Procedure inputs and output

Logo procedures can be thought of as jigsaw puzzle pieces, and our job as programmers is to build puzzles which fit together properly. The procedures that we will build, and the built-in procedures that come with MicroWorlds, have a specified number of inputs. It can be zero inputs (such as **pd**) or one input (such as **forward**) or more inputs (such as **sum**). A procedure can also have zero outputs (such as **forward**) or one output (such as **sum**).

A procedure that needs no inputs is simply a square jigsaw puzzle piece. One that needs one input has a hole on the right for a tab. The output puzzle piece next to it has a tab sticking out on the left. So they fit together. When we use procedures in an instruction we must provide the required inputs and we must provide a place for the outputs to go, in order for the whole instruction to be correct. Think of it as a one-line jigsaw puzzle.

Here are two procedures:

As you can see, forward has a hole that needs a number input and, of course, 50 has a number output that will fit just fine.

Procedures that expect one number as their input will have the right size opening to fit a number. In fact, a number is really a procedure with one output (the number) and no inputs.

The starting edge of a line of instruction must be solid, that is no output sticking out, and so must the ending edge.

Here are some instructions. Try to guess which ones will work and which ones won't.

Type them into the Command Center to test your guess.

Instruction 1

Instruction 2

Instruction 3

Instruction 4

It's really pretty easy to get the inputs and outputs all lined up and in the right order once you pretend the procedures are jigsaw pieces and the instruction must be a completed puzzle!

If an instruction is going to work, then all the openings and tabs must be used. Note that this means that an instruction can't begin with a procedure that has an output.

Programming with style

A computer program has to achieve more than just doing the job. It needs to have staying power—meaning that it needs to be easily understood and changed by others. Here are some goals to keep in mind when writing a program:

1. Set up the plan of attack ahead of time.
2. Use small, one-purpose-only procedures whenever possible. This makes it easy for someone to change it later.
3. Document your work so the next person can understand it.
4. The code must work every time for every one.
5. Choose consistent, sensible names for procedures.

Where to write your program?

First, let's talk about where *not* to write your program. If you right-click on a turtle, you see a dialog box or "backpack" which allows you to enter your instruction for the turtle. This is NOT a good idea! Goal number 2 above says that the program must be easily read. How can it be easily read if instructions are scattered all over the place with individual turtles? The dialog boxes that are associated with the controls such as turtles and buttons are not where you want to hide your beautifully crafted code.

In MicroWorlds 2.0, you must click on the Pages menu at the top of the screen, and then click on Procedures. You are presented with a blank page. This is where as much of your code as possible belongs. We can toggle back and forth between the procedures page and page1 where the turtle is drawing, by pushing **ctrl** and **f** at the same time.

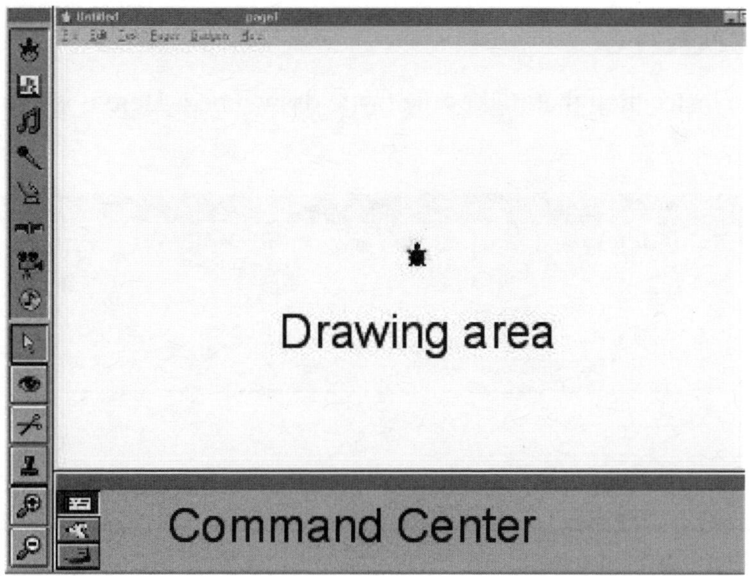

MicroWorlds 2.0 main screen. Use Pages menu at the top to go to the Procedures Page.

In MicroWorlds EX, the procedures "page" or window is to the right alongside the drawing "page," provided the Procedures tab beneath it is selected. The Command Center is to the bottom left.

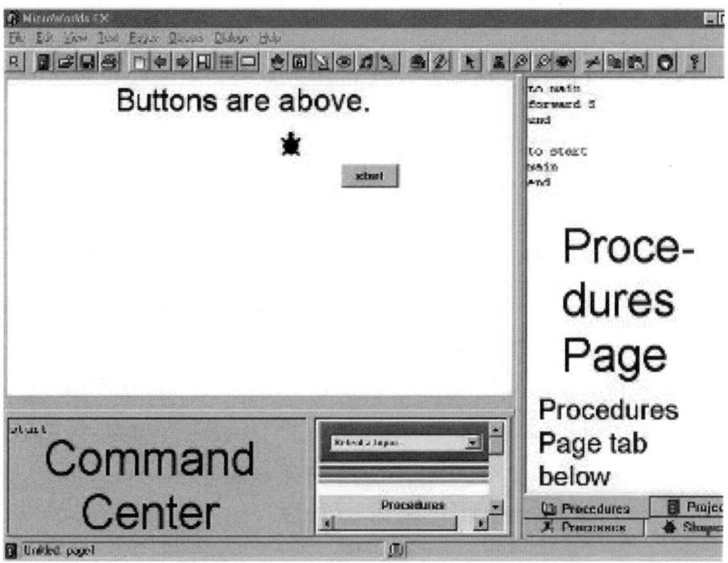

MicroWorlds EX main screen

Write a procedure

Okay, we now have an instruction that makes the turtle draw a box. Here it is again:

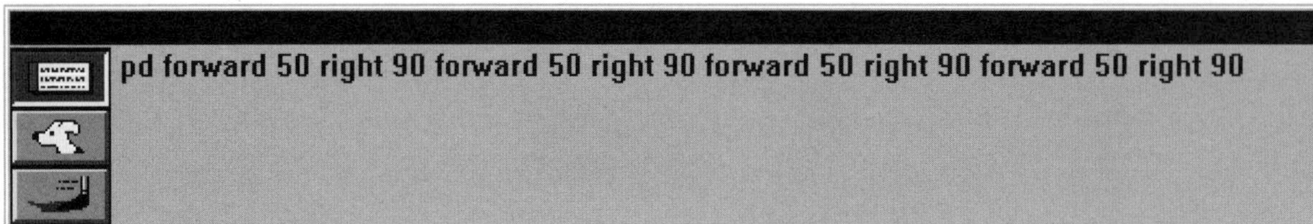

Our beginning project is to develop procedures that make the turtle move in a variety of ways. If we left off the instruction **pd** (pen down), then we would have an instruction to make the turtle move in a square. Let's make that our first procedure.

You can teach MicroWorlds new words by writing procedures. Remember our instructions for setting the table? Let's write a "procedure" for that.

To SetTheTable
get a plate from the cupboard
walk to the table
put it on the table
return to the cupboard
get a glass
... and so on
end

You give the person you are teaching a list of instructions using words that she knows. You are, in a way, teaching her a new phrase, "set the table."

Now we are going to write a set of detailed instructions for MicroWorlds to draw a square. This is the essence of programming, namely adding new procedures and capabilities to the existing ones that came with the language.

What shall we call our new word? How about **square**. Then, when we want the turtle to move in the shape of a square, we can just type **square**, instead of that long instruction we developed above.

On the procedures page, type the following:

```
to square
  pd forward 50 right 90 forward 50 right 90 forward 50 right 90 forward 50 right 90
end
```

All procedures start with the word **to** and end with the word **end.** A procedure like this adds a new word to MicroWorlds vocabulary. It uses **pd**, which puts the turtle's "pen" down, **forward 50**, which moves the turtle 50 "steps" in the direction it is facing, and **right 90,** which turns the turtle to the right by 90 degrees. Let's try it out! Press **Ctrl-F** to return to the program page. In the Command Center, type **cc** to clear the command center and push **Enter** if you need to clean out old messages. Then type **square** and press Enter.

Hmm, mine didn't work very well. I think the problem is that the turtle went so fast, you couldn't see it.

It is very common that things don't work quite right the first time. This is not a failure, it just means we can tweak our procedure to make it better!

Before we slow the movement down, there is another problem with our **square** procedure. As it is now, it is not really very readable. Let's write the same long instruction over many lines, making it much more readable. We can do that on the procedure page whereas it is not as easy in the command center, or heaven forbid, a dialog box. MicroWorlds Logo just ignores the fact that the instruction is spread over many pages. MicroWorlds Logo is really just interested in whether the inputs and outputs are all satisfied.

Change your procedure so it looks like this:

```
to square
  pd
  forward 50 right 90
  forward 50 right 90
  forward 50 right 90
  forward 50 right 90
end
```

There, that is much more readable and you can see at a glance how it works. Notice that our procedure **square** takes no inputs and has no output so its puzzle piece looks like this:

It is a "satisfied" instruction all by itself.
Now back to improving our first procedure. To slow the movement of the turtle down, let's add a built-in procedure, **wait**, after each turn that the turtle makes. **Wait** takes one input, a number. Change your procedure so it looks like this:

```
to square
  pd
  forward 50 right 90 wait 1
  forward 50 right 90 wait 1
  forward 50 right 90 wait 1
  forward 50 right 90 wait 1
end
```

Hit **Ctrl-F** and we'll give it a try! We type **square** in the command center.

Does it work? Here are some general troubleshooting hints: be sure each procedure begins with **to** and ends with **end**. Make sure what you typed exactly matches what we are telling you to type.

Hey, that's much better. On the last line of the **square** procedure, you see that **wait 1** is there, even though the movement of the turtle is finished. We could remove this last **wait 1** but there is little to gain, and later we may want to use this procedure to make the turtle move round and round the square many times. In that case having the **wait 1** will make the movement even.

Let's add a comment to let any future readers know what this procedure does **(Goal 3)**. We'll make a second line like this: **;draws a square of 50 units**

```
to square
   ;draws a square of 50 units
   pd
   forward 50 right 90 wait 1
   forward 50 right 90 wait 1
   forward 50 right 90 wait 1
   forward 50 right 90 wait 1
end
```

Now we have a procedure to be proud of, but we still don't have a program.

So that you can continue with this project at another time, please save your work as **Starter.** Put it in a folder called My Documents, if there isn't another one for student work.

Show your teacher that you have saved your class work and that it draws a square.

Assignment 1: Write a set of instructions with at least eight lines to describe all the steps, in order, for doing a chore that you do regularly.

#3 A Simple Logo Program

Load in your work

From the file menu, open your project named **Starter.** We will make some changes to this file, and we want to keep an unchanged version, so we need another copy. From the file menu select "Save Project As" and save your project as **Square.**

Let's talk for a minute about what is going on when you save a file. The computer filing system is like a filing cabinet, in a way. Think of a file as being like a piece of paper with writing on it. You can save a bunch of these files in a "folder." Think of a "folder" as being like a manila folder. You can put a bunch of folders in a big folder. There are three big file drawers, which hold all the folders and folders inside of folders. One is called A:. This is your floppy disk drive. It can hold some information, not much really, on a floppy disk. The next is called C: This is your hard drive, which remains permanently inside your computer. This is probably your biggest storage area. And there is the D: drive, your CD-ROM drive. This is a special type of "read-only-memory," which you can pull out and load but you can't change. (Regular storage memory is for both reading and writing, or changing.)

While we're talking about it, there's the computer "desktop." This is supposed to emulate (pretend to be) your real desk, with file folders sitting out on it ready for you to pick up and work with.

Find your Procedures page. It should look like this:

```
to square
   ;draws a square of 50 units
   pd
   forward 50 right 90 wait 1
   forward 50 right 90 wait 1
   forward 50 right 90 wait 1
   forward 50 right 90 wait 1
end
```

Making a simple program

The Command Center makes a perfect place to test instructions and procedures. But it is not a very user-friendly place from which to launch a program. Also, later when we make stand-alone programs to run on a Web page, the Command Center doesn't show. So we need to learn to do without it.

Our program page is the page where the turtle draws squares for us. We need a button right on our program page. To get there, go to the page menu, and then to page1. Click the button icon (it looks like a finger pushing a button), and then click on the program page. A dialog box pops up. Looking at it you can see that we are allowed to type in an instruction to be run when someone clicks on the button.

We want to wire this button so it starts our program.

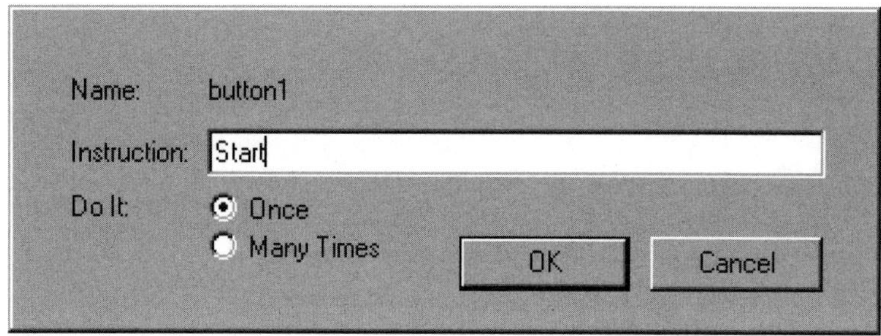

In the instruction box, type **Start** and click OK. (In MicroWorlds EX, you can also provide the name of the button. Name it **Start** as well.) Then drag the button so it fits nice and tight in the bottom left corner of page1.

I suggest you save your work often. On a PC, if you press two keys ctrl and s together, it will save the revised project under the name you just gave, **Square.**

Now click on the **Start** button. We get the error message "I don't know how to Start." This is exactly what we are going to teach MicroWorlds now!

To get quickly back to the Procedures page, strike two keys at the same time, **<ctrl>** and **f**. Remember this shortcut!! You will use it a lot. Now, to add the word **Start** to MicroWorlds' vocabulary, we need to make a **Start** procedure.

First I would like to comment on program design. Remember these lessons are to teach you good programming techniques. They are not just to teach you about MicroWorlds or Logo. The computer language C is a favorite professional language and so is C++. Both of these languages, in particular C++, have been designed to help programmers manage the complexity of computer programs and both of these languages start every program's execution at a procedure named **Main**. This means that the first procedure to run is always called **Main**. If you are reading a program in C or C++, you would typically start by looking for the procedure named **Main**. I feel it is a very good convention to follow.

So we will make a **Start** procedure which will call (run) our **Main** procedure. Add these to your procedures page:

```
to Start
  Main
end

to Main
  cc
  talkto "t1
  ;works with turtle named t1
  repeat 20 [Square]
end
```

Save your work by striking **<ctrl>** and **s**.

We now have a complete program! Main tells the computer what to do first, then next, and so on. The procedures after it tell the computer how to do the commands it doesn't know already.

The first instruction in **Main** tells MicroWorlds to clear the command center. This is so we know that any error messages we see are new ones. The next instruction in **Main** tells MicroWorlds which turtle should perform the actions in the following instructions. It is not necessary to have that instruction if there is only one turtle, but it improves the readability of our program, which is one of our goals.

The third line uses the built-in procedure **repeat** which requires two inputs: a number indicating how many repetitions, and a list of instructions to repeat. We only have one instruction, ***so to make it into a list you just put square brackets around it.*** We will be talking more about lists later.

Try running your program by going to page1 and clicking the **Start** button. Now try running it in Presentation Mode by going to the **Gadgets** menu (or **View** menu in MicroWorlds EX) and clicking on **Presentation Mode.** Then click the Start button. To get out of Presentation Mode, double-click on the black border.

One final bit of house cleaning to do. As this and other programs grow, your procedures page gets very large. So you don't waste time looking for procedures, you should keep them in alphabetical order. To move procedures around, highlight the lines of text by putting the mouse button down next to them, holding it down, and moving the cursor to the other side of them. Now go to he Edit menu, and select cut. The lines seem to vanish. Really you have put them on an invisible clipboard. Now move the cursor where you want the lines to be, and select edit, then paste. Presto, the lines show up in the new spot! This cut and paste routine works in nearly all computer applications. You can also use copy and paste if you want to make copies somewhere else.

I usually do something special with **Main** to make it particularly easy to find, such as type double lines before and after it. By the way, MicroWorlds is not case-sensitive, so it doesn't matter if you type capital or lower-case letters. Here is my Procedures Page:

```
====================
to Main
   cc
   talkto "t1
   ;works with turtle named t1
   repeat 20 [Square]
end
====================
to square
   ;draws a square of 50 units
   pd
   forward 50 right 90 wait 1
   forward 50 right 90 wait 1
   forward 50 right 90 wait 1
   forward 50 right 90 wait 1
end
```

```
to Start
   Main
end
```

Can you figure out how to rewrite your **square** procedure using **repeat**? Remember **repeat** needs two inputs, a number indicating how many repetitions, and a list of instructions to repeat.

So that you can continue with this project at another time, please save your work under its current name, **Square,** by striking **<ctrl> s**. ***Run*** your program for a teacher, and ***show*** you have proper format on the procedures page.

If you have time, let's play with it:

- Repeat the instruction in **square** three rather than four times. Press **Start** repeatedly. What happens?
- Make larger squares.
- Wait longer.
- Try a different angle and see what you draw.

(After you make any of these changes, save it under a different name, such as **mysquare**). We will be pulling up **Square** later and want it to be a clean copy.)

#4 Logo Running Horse

From the file menu, open your project named **Square**. Then from the file menu select "Save Project As" and save your project as **Square1.**

In the procedures page, make sure your program looks like this:

```
====================
to Main
   cc
   talkto "t1
   ;works with turtle named t1
   repeat 20 [square]
end
====================

to square
   ;draws a square of 50 units
   pd
   repeat 4 [forward 50 right 90 wait 1]
end

to start
   Main
end
```

Play with your creation

Try experimenting with your program. Go to the Shape Center at the bottom of the MicroWorlds 2.0 page by clicking on the blue dog head next to the Command Center. (In MicroWorlds EX, click on the Shapes tab on the lower right.[2])

In the Shape Center, click on a shape and then on the turtle. Click on the Start Button. It doesn't matter what shape the turtle is wearing. He still goes around and around in a square. Notice that

---

[2] MicroWorlds EX shapes: If you are using MicroWorlds EX, you will need to import shapes from the drawing/painting window to your shape center before doing this project or others with non-turtle shapes. Click on the icon at the top that looks like a yellow and purple paintbrush. The drawing/painting window opens up. Click on the daisy icon to see the single shapes, or the two-people icon to see animation shapes. Now drag the drawing window over to the left by clicking down on the blue band at the top, and holding the mouse button down, dragging sideways. Make sure the window on the right is the shape center by clicking on the tab beneath it that says "shapes." Drag individual shapes from the drawing/painting window to the shapes window. Once a shape is "installed" in this way, you can use it in your programs. For this lesson you will need to install and use horse5, horse6 and horse7 instead of horse1, horse2, and horse3, as described in the text for MicroWorlds 2.0. Later you will need doggy1 and doggy2 instead of dog1 and dog2 as used in the text. You will also need to substitute other shapes when you can't find the shape described in the text for MicroWorlds 2.0. Don't be discouraged; the EX shapes are very nice!

although the turtle's head rotates with the direction it is traveling, the other shapes it can wear do not. So to see which way the turtle is facing, you have to change it back to a turtle shape.

Adjust the amount the turtle moves forward in the procedure **square.** Change the size of the turtle shape with the magnifying glass.

It would be nice if the turtle could be programmed to automatically change shapes. With MicroWorlds this is actually very easy. There is a built-in procedure called **setsh** which stands for set shape. It requires an input which is either a word (must be the name of a shape) or a list of words (must be a list of names of shapes). Here is an example of both:

```
setsh "horse1
setsh [horse1 horse2 horse3]
```

Why do I need to put the quotation mark in front of **"horse1**? Why not just **setsh horse1**?

When you give MicroWorlds Logo a word, like **start** or **main** or **setsh or horse1**, it assumes the word is a procedure to look up in its vocabulary and run. It treats it as an action word, or a verb. Putting the quotes in front says, "This is a name of something; don't try to run it." It says it's a noun.

So without the quotes in front of **horse1**, MicroWorlds will try to run the procedure **horse1**. But naturally, there isn't one.

Go to the Command Center and type **horse1** and press Enter. See, it tries to 'run' **horse1** but doesn't know how to. However, in the instruction **setsh "horse1**, because the word is quoted, MicroWorlds Logo knows that you mean the name of something, and treats it just as a name word and not something it needs to do.

Make sure the " is made by one stroke of the key next to the semicolon key, while holding down the shift key. Two strokes of the ' key won't do.

Setsh needs either a word or a list of words as its input. So, **setsh "horse1** is a complete instruction. In the second example, **setsh [horse1 horse2 horse3],** you don't have to quote each name because the brackets show that it is a list. **Setsh** is known to accept as its input a list of names of shapes. Therefore MicroWorlds knows to interpret the words as a list of shape names.

Change your **Main** procedure to look like this:

```
to Main
   cc
   talkto "t1
   ;works with turtle named t1
   setsh [horse1 horse2 horse3]
   repeat 20 [square]
end
```

What do you think will happen? Go back to your program and try it. Surprise! The horse is running around a square! (See troubleshooting suggestions in the Appendix if you need to.)

Why is the horse running around a square? MicroWorlds Logo has a neat feature where if you set up a list of shapes ahead of time with **setsh**, as we did, each time the procedure **forward** or **back** is called, a new shape from the list is used. Remember that our **square** procedure uses **forward** repeatedly, so each time it uses forward, the shape of the turtle changes to the next one on the list. As the shapes change quickly, the turtle (which now looks like a horse facing to the right) seems to be running. This is simple animation!! You've probably seen a lot of it, and now you know how it works!

Do these:

Turn your turtle turn into a running dog using **dog1** and **dog2** (in MicroWorlds EX, **doggy1** and **doggy2**).

Pull the pen up so the square isn't seen. Use the command **pu**, for pen up.

Make the horse or dog run in a straight line, not a square. (Don't change the **square** procedure; just don't call it. Replace the line in **Main** that calls it with another command.)

Increase the wait time after the **forward** command, to slow the animation down.

Is your horse or dog levitating? Running backward? Make sure the horse or dog is running the same direction it is facing. In **Main**, change the direction it moves using **seth**, for set heading. (A "heading" is the direction a boat is facing, for example north.) The number is a number of degrees, a measure of how much the horse-turtle is turning. **Seth 0** points the turtle's head upward. **Seth 90** points its head to the right. **Seth –90** (or **seth 270**) points it to the left. **Seth 180** points it down.

Or, in Microworlds 2.0 you can flip the horse or dog to face the other way by double clicking on its shape in the shape center (get there by clicking on the dog head next to the command center) and then clicking the reverse icon. But this is not as good a solution to the problem because it doesn't meet our programming goal which says, "The code must work every time for every one." The code doesn't work if the shape is facing the wrong way, so we ought to change the code, not the shape.

Save your work

Hit **control-s** to save your work under the name you had given it. ***Show*** your teacher that the horse or dog runs in a straight line, not too fast, without drawing a line. Make sure that on the procedures page, the Main procedure comes first and is set off by double lines, and that the other procedures are in alphabetical order.

#5 Simple Logo House

Open up **Square**. It should look like this:

```
====================
to Main
   cc
   talkto "t1
   ;works with turtle named t1
   repeat 20 [Square]
end
====================

to square
   ;draws a square of 50 units
   pd
   repeat 4 [forward 50 right 90 wait 1]
end

to start
   Main
end
```

Now save it as **House**. This makes a copy of it that we will change.

So far we have only been drawing a square. Let's do some experimenting to see if we can draw a triangle. Go to the command center on page1 and type **cc <enter>**, to clear the command center, then **cg <enter>** to clear the graphics.

First, let's talk about degrees. Degrees measure how much you are turning. We have discussed already that a 90-degree turn is the measure of a right angle. When the turtle draws a square, it makes 90-degree turns. But how much is a degree, anyway? In the Command Center, let's tell our turtle to put its pen down, turn one degree, go forward 50 and back 50.

```
cg
pd right 1 forward 50 back 50
```

Hmm. Obviously one degree isn't much. Now, what if we tell it to repeat those same commands 45 times?

```
repeat 45 [ right 1 forward 50 back 50]
```

90 times? Enough times to go full circle? Experiment until your turtle is drawing a starburst. Remember **repeat** has two inputs: a number of times to repeat, and a list of commands to repeat. You have just learned that there are 360 degrees in a circle, and each degree is a tiny turn for the turtle.

Now, about going through the turns to draw a figure. Let's suppose YOU are a turtle, and the floor of the room you are in is the screen. If you are facing straight ahead and then turn yourself to face to the right, you have turned yourself 90 degrees.

Now choose three endpoints for a big equal-sided triangle on the floor (for example, a chair, the door jamb, and a table leg.) Walk along one side of the triangle, and then turn yourself the required angle to get to the next side. You have turned more than 90 degrees! In fact, you have turned 120 degrees. Go to the next corner. Turn 120 degrees. Walk to the next corner. Turn 120 degrees. You are now facing the same way you started, so you have turned a total of 360 degrees, or full circle. You have now done all the turns that a turtle would do if it were drawing an equal-sided, or equilateral, triangle.

Now draw a triangle with a pencil on a piece of paper. Suppose that it is 50 turtle steps on a side. Write a set of instructions in English on a piece of paper that tells the turtle how far to walk and how far to turn. Then translate it to Logo. Use **repeat. (Check this and other answers near the end of the book. Also find a troubleshooting guide there.)**

Get to the procedures page (using <ctrl f> in MicroWorlds 2.0)**.** Name our new procedure **To triangle**. Add a line of explanation, such as **;draws a triangle of 50 units.** Don't forget **pd.** Then type in your instructions. Finish with **end**.

In MicroWorlds 2.0, use **<ctrl> f** to get back to page1. In the Command Center, type **triangle** and hit enter. Did the turtle draw a triangle? Go back to the procedures page**.** Adjust the procedure till it works. Show your teacher that it works by going to the Command Center and typing **triangle <enter>.**

We can draw a lot more than triangles. In the Command Center, play with turns of smaller angles. We'll see what happens with **right 60** instead of **right 120**, just for grins. Type in this:

```
cg
pd
repeat 8 [forward 50 right 60 wait 1]
```

and press **<enter>**. What happened? Now replace **right 60** with **right 30**, then **right 20**, then **right 1**. You'll need to increase the number of repeats to get a good idea of what you are drawing. To return the turtle to its centered, heads-up position, type **cg,** then **pd.**

Here's another tool you will need for a bigger drawing: pen up, or **pu**. Your turtle will be crawling around and drawing things. If you don't want a line to follow him, pull his pen up, move to another spot, and then put it down again (**pd**).

Now, let's work on calling our square and triangle procedures to make a simple picture of a house: a square with triangle on top.

Returning to the command center, let's try this:

> **cg**
> **square**
> **triangle**

What did the turtle draw? It doesn't look like a house. What is wrong?

Our turtle needs to clear graphics, draw a square making right turns, pick its pen up, then move up to the roof and face along one line of the triangle before it starts making right turns to draw the roof triangle. Imagine you are the turtle and write down instructions in English using a piece of paper. Translate them to Logo. What combination of **pu, forward** and **right** will do the trick? Here's another function you may need: **seth**, for set heading. Remember that **seth 0** points the turtle up; **seth 90** points it to the right; **seth –90** points it to the left; **seth 180** points it down.

Then type them into the procedures page. To test them, go to the Command Center and type the name of the procedure.

Name this procedure **climb.to.roof,** which MicroWorlds reads as all one word, a name. Don't forget the beginning and end words, and a line of explanation.

On the procedures page, create another procedure called **to house** that explains what it is doing, clears graphics, and then calls the procedures **square, climb.to.roof**, and **triangle.** End it with **end.**

Save your work using **<ctrl> s**, as **House.** ***Show*** your teacher that your program draws a house when you type **house <enter>** in the command center.

Assignment--prepare for Skyscraper Project:

With a pencil, draw an interesting building of at least five stories with at least three different architectural elements (door, window, porch). It can have a number of windows the same size, or two doors the same size.

#6 Add to Logo House

Open **House,** and rename it as **House1.** Let's make some improvements to our house.

We'll start with a door. We'd like the door to be somewhere in the front wall of the house, which we remember is 50 units long. Let's write ourselves some instructions in English first. Remember that the turtle is at the upper left side of the square, facing upward and toward the right along the roof line, when it has finished drawing the house. Where to now? How about if we:

pick the pen up
face downward
climb down from the roof to the ground
and turn to face to the right (using seth).

Then we can move forward say 20 units

put the pen down
turn to face upward again
and draw a door. (This will take a combination of forward and turn commands.)

First, make a sketch of your house showing its measurements. This will help you envision how far the turtle has to go, and how much it turns.

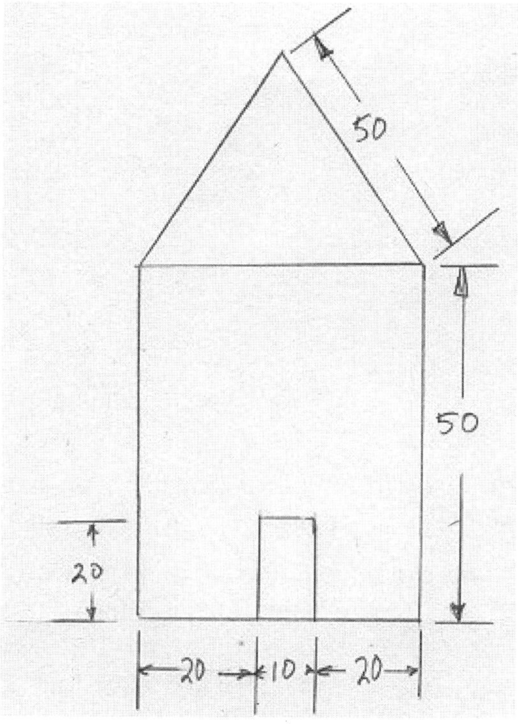

Make your list of commands in English on paper first. When you can pretend to be a turtle and follow them, it's time to translate into Logo and type them into the command center to see if they work. When they do, copy them and paste them onto the procedures page. Make procedures called **move.to.door** and **door**, and call them from **house.** When it is working properly, show your teacher. Save your work using **<ctrl> s** under the name you already gave it.

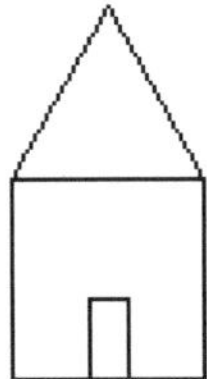

Here is what it may look like.

Now, make a window. Start with a drawing again:

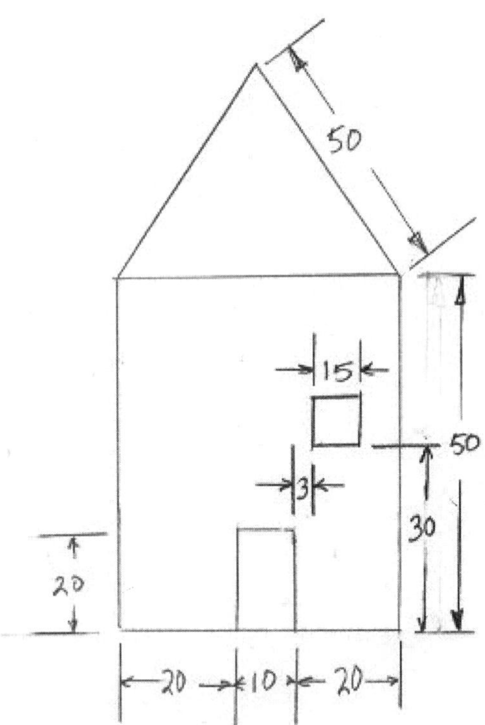

Write code that moves the turtle along the measurements that you are seeing in your drawing. Make another window and a chimney on your own. If you have time, add stairs.

Color your house. Here's how you do it: you imagine that the turtle carries a bucket of paint with it. You assign the color in that bucket using **setc** (for set color) with a number input, for example **setc 15** fills the bucket with red. You can also use the name of the color, as an input, if you do it with a quote mark like this: **setc "red** . (Find other colors by trial and error, or by using the help menu. Or pause the pointer arrow over a color in the drawing center in MicroWorlds 2.0, and in MicroWorlds EX right-click on a color in the painting window.)

You can make a procedure called **colorhouse**. In it, pick the pen up (pu), move the turtle a few steps into the space you want to color, assign a color using **setc,** and using the built-in command **fill** to "dump the bucket." For example:

```
to colorhouse
    pu
    forward 30
    setc 15
    fill
end
```

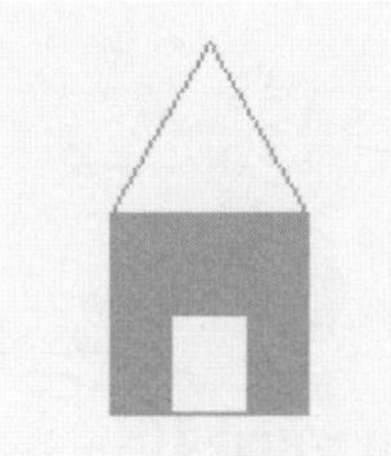

When the house program is working properly, ***show*** your teacher. Save your work using **<ctrl> s** under the name you already gave it.

Skyscraper project assignment:

Take your drawing of a big building. Put measurements on it, like we did on our house drawing. Now, make some instructions in English for drawing it. Make a Main procedure that describes how to draw the building in just a few lines in English. (For example: draw the outline, move the turtle, draw the door, move the turtle, draw a window, move the turtle ...). Then for each of those lines, make a procedure that says in detail how to draw one of those in English. Remember, our goals call for procedures that have one purpose only.

#7 Logo Skyscraper Project

Now it is time to draw the big skyscraper!

If you have done your assignments, you have made a careful drawing of a skyscraper designed by you. You have a list of how to do it, in English. Now you need to translate to Logo.

You have the tools you need to do this, except for the concept of a row of windows. To make a row of windows, create a procedure called **windowrow**. In it, use the repeat function to repeatedly draw a window plus the space between it and the next window. For instance, **window** and **windowrow** could look like this:

```
to window
   seth 0
   pd
   repeat 4 [forward 5 right 90]
end

to windowrow
   repeat 15 [pd window seth 90 pu forward 10]
end
```

Start a new file for this project. You can name it YourInitials Building. Write your main procedure first. This will serve as a list of procedures that you will create, for example:

```
to Main
  cg
  movedown
  outline
  move1
  door
  move2
  windowrow
end
```

Now you need to write the first of these procedures and test it. You can do this in the Command Center, where you can watch the turtle moving as you type in commands. First create a set of commands that draws your outline. Then highlight them, **copy** them using the **edit** menu, and **paste** them on the procedures page. Add a procedure name.

For example, your **outline** commands in the Command Center might look like this:

```
seth 0
pd
repeat 2 [forward 150 right 90 forward 50 right 90]
pu
```

So you copy those to the procedures page and put "**to outline**" at the top, and "**end**" at the bottom, and you have a procedure. You can call the procedure from the Command Center by typing its name there. Remember to make procedures that do one thing (draw an outline) not two (such as move to a spot and draw an outline). Add a comment (starting with "**;**") to each procedure telling what it does. Test it by typing **outline** in the Command Center and pressing **enter**.

Now write the next procedure, test it, and so on. Look for chances to use the built-in procedure **repeat**, which can repeat any procedure that you write. Also, don't forget **pd** and **pu** as you move the turtle around.

As you work, remember our goals for programming with style:

1. Set up the plan of attack ahead of time.
2. Use small, one-purpose-only procedures whenever possible. This makes it easy for someone to change it later.
3. Document your work so the next person can understand it.
4. The code must work every time for every one.
5. Choose consistent, sensible names for procedures.

Continue improving your building whenever you have time—add steps, porches. See the troubleshooting guide in the appendix if you need to. Work on a second building, or other enhancements to a cityscape. How about a bridge? A newsstand? A tree? You will have several class periods to work on this. See the requirements below for the project you will turn in.

Skyscraper Project Requirements

Requirements:

- Your program works.
- Your building must have an outline plus at least three different features (window, door, antenna).
- Procedures do one thing (draw a window or move to another spot, but not both).
- Each procedure contains a comment, for example, **";moves up and over to the next window position."**
- Main is set off by double lines. Other procedures are in alphabetical order.
- Other features, including color and a start button, will give extra credit.

#8 More Word Processing

In this lesson, let's learn to format a newsletter and also look at a broad view of what our word processor can do.

A newsletter

First, let's format a newsletter. We need to input a bunch of words or pseudo-words. You may have a file with lots of words in it. Or you can make some dummy words for this exercise. For example, you could type this line: xxx xxx xxxxx xxxxx x xxxxxxxx xxx xxx. Then you could highlight it, and go to **Edit**, then **Copy**. Now it is on your invisible "clipboard." You can make enough repetitions of it to fill up a page by simply hitting **Paste** or **control-v** over and over again.

```
:··xxx·xxx·xxxxx·xxxxx·x·xxxxxxxx·xxx·xxx.·:··xxx·xxx·xxxxx·xxxxx·x·xxxxxxxx·xxx·
xxx.·:··xxx·xxx·xxxxx·xxxxx·x·xxxxxxxx·xxx·xxx.·:··xxx·xxx·xxxxx·xxxxx·x·xxxxxxxx·
xxx·xxx.·:··xxx·xxx·xxxxx·xxxxx·x·xxxxxxxx·xxx·xxx.·:··xxx·xxx·xxxxx·xxxxx·x·
xxxxxxxx·xxx·xxx.·:··xxx·xxx·xxxxx·xxxxx·x·xxxxxxxx·xxx·xxx.·:··xxx·xxx·xxxxx·
xxxxx·x·xxxxxxxx·xxx·xxx.·:··xxx·xxx·xxxxx·xxxxx·x·xxxxxxxx·xxx·xxx.·:··xxx·xxx·
xxxxx·xxxxx·x·xxxxxxxx·xxx·xxx.·:··xxx·xxx·xxxxx·xxxxx·x·xxxxxxxx·xxx·xxx.·:··xxx·
xxx·xxxxx·xxxxx·x·xxxxxxxx·xxx·xxx.·:··xxx·xxx·xxxxx·xxxxx·x·xxxxxxxx·xxx·xxx.·:··
xxx·xxx·xxxxx·xxxxx·x·xxxxxxxx·xxx·xxx.·:··xxx·xxx·xxxxx·xxxxx·x·xxxxxxxx·xxx·
xxx.·:··xxx·xxx·xxxxx·xxxxx·x·xxxxxxxx·xxx·xxx.·:··xxx·xxx·xxxxx·xxxxx·x·xxxxxxxx·
xxx·xxx.·:··xxx·xxx·xxxxx·xxxxx·x·xxxxxxxx·xxx·xxx.·:··xxx·xxx·xxxxx·xxxxx·x·
xxxxxxxx·xxx·xxx.·:··xxx·xxx·xxxxx·xxxxx·x·xxxxxxxx·xxx·xxx.·:··xxx·xxx·xxxxx·
xxxxx·x·xxxxxxxx·xxx·xxx.·:··xxx·xxx·xxxxx·xxxxx·x·xxxxxxxx·xxx·xxx.·:··xxx·xxx·
xxxxx·xxxxx·x·xxxxxxxx·xxx·xxx.·:··xxx·xxx·xxxxx·xxxxx·x·xxxxxxxx·xxx·xxx.·:··xxx·
xxx·xxxxx·xxxxx·x·xxxxxxxx·xxx·xxx.·:··xxx·xxx·xxxxx·xxxxx·x·xxxxxxxx·xxx·xxx.·:··
xxx·xxx·xxxxx·xxxxx·x·xxxxxxxx·xxx·xxx.·:··xxx·xxx·xxxxx·xxxxx·x·xxxxxxxx·xxx·
xxx.·:··xxx·xxx·xxxxx·xxxxx·x·xxxxxxxx·xxx·xxx.·:··xxx·xxx·xxxxx·xxxxx·x·xxxxxxxx·
xxx·xxx.·:··xxx·xxx·xxxxx·xxxxx·x·xxxxxxxx·xxx·xxx.·:··xxx·xxx·xxxxx·xxxxx·x·
xxxxxxxx·xxx·xxx.·:··xxx·xxx·xxxxx·xxxxx·x·xxxxxxxx·xxx·xxx.·:··xxx·xxx·xxxxx·
xxxxx·x·xxxxxxxx·xxx·xxx.·:··xxx·xxx·xxxxx·xxxxx·x·xxxxxxxx·xxx·xxx.·:··xxx·xxx·
xxxxx·xxxxx·x·xxxxxxxx·xxx·xxx.·:··xxx·xxx·xxxxx·xxxxx·x·xxxxxxxx·xxx·xxx.·:··xxx·
xxx·xxxxx·xxxxx·x·xxxxxxxx·xxx·xxx.·:··xxx·xxx·xxxxx·xxxxx·x·xxxxxxxx·xxx·xxx.·:··
xxx·xxx·xxxxx·xxxxx·x·xxxxxxxx·xxx·xxx.·:··xxx·xxx·xxxxx·xxxxx·x·xxxxxxxx·xxx·
xxx.¶
```

Now, highlight all these "words" and click on the columns icon: . Or, if you can't find it, go to the **Format** menu, then **Columns**. Select two columns. Now it looks like this:

```
x·xxxxxxxx·xxx·xxx.·:··xxx·xxx·xxxxx·
xxxxx·x·xxxxxxxx·xxx·xxx.·:··xxx·xxx·
xxxxx·xxxxx·x·xxxxxxxx·xxx·xxx.·:··
xxx·xxx·xxxxx·xxxxx·x·xxxxxxxx·xxx·
xxx.·:··xxx·xxx·xxxxx·xxxxx·x·
xxxxxxxx·xxx·xxx.·:··xxx·xxx·xxxxx·
xxxxx·x·xxxxxxxx·xxx·xxx.·:··xxx·xxx·
xxxxx·xxxxx·x·xxxxxxxx·xxx·xxx.·:··
xxx·xxx·xxxxx·xxxxx·x·xxxxxxxx·xxx·
xxx.·:··xxx·xxx·xxxxx·xxxxx·x·
```

```
xxxxx·xxxxx·x·xxxxxxxx·xxx·xxx.·:··
xxx·xxx·xxxxx·xxxxx·x·xxxxxxxx·xxx·
xxx.·:··xxx·xxx·xxxxx·xxxxx·x·
xxxxxxxx·xxx·xxx.·:··xxx·xxx·xxxxx·
xxxxx·x·xxxxxxxx·xxx·xxx.·:··xxx·xxx·
xxxxx·xxxxx·x·xxxxxxxx·xxx·xxx.·:··
xxx·xxx·xxxxx·xxxxx·x·xxxxxxxx·xxx·
xxx.·:··xxx·xxx·xxxxx·xxxxx·x·
xxxxxxxx·xxx·xxx.·:··xxx·xxx·xxxxx·
xxxxx·x·xxxxxxxx·xxx·xxx.·:··xxx·xxx·
```

What if your "document" looks lopsided like this?

```
:··xxx·xxx·xxxxx·xxxxx·x·xxxxxxxx·xxx·      xxx.·:··xxx·xxx·xxxxx·xxxxx·x·
xxx.·:··xxx·xxx·xxxxx·xxxxx·x·              xxxxxxxx·xxx·xxx.·:··xxx·xxx·xxxxx·
xxxxxxxx·xxx·xxx.·:··xxx·xxx·xxxxx·         xxxxx·x·xxxxxxxx·xxx·xxx.·:··xxx·xxx·
xxxxx·x·xxxxxxxx·xxx·xxx.·:··xxx·xxx·       xxxxx·xxxxx·x·xxxxxxxx·xxx·xxx.·:··
xxxxx·xxxxx·x·xxxxxxxx·xxx·xxx.·:··         xxx·xxx·xxxxx·xxxxx·x·xxxxxxxx·xxx·¶
xxx·xxx·xxxxx·xxxxx·x·xxxxxxxx·xxx·
xxx.·:··xxx·xxx·xxxxx·xxxxx·x·
xxxxxxxx·xxx·xxx.·:··xxx·xxx·xxxxx·
xxxxx·x·xxxxxxxx·xxx·xxx.·:··xxx·xxx·
xxxxx·xxxxx·x·xxxxxxxx·xxx·xxx.·:··
xxx·xxx·xxxxx·xxxxx·x·xxxxxxxx·xxx·
xxx.·:··xxx·xxx·xxxxx·xxxxx·x·
xxxxxxxx·xxx·xxx.·:··xxx·xxx·xxxxx·
xxxxx·x·xxxxxxxx·xxx·xxx.·:··xxx·xxx·
xxxxx·xxxxx·x·xxxxxxxx·xxx·xxx.·:··
```

Then you need to make sure you insert a section break at the end. Put your cursor at the end, and go to the **Insert** menu, then **Break**, then select **continuous section break**. This is a marker for the computer that separates different areas of your document, such as the headline from the body text, and two-column sections from one-column sections.

In order to see your section break, and also any paragraph marks, you need to click on the show-hide button, ¶. This shows otherwise-invisible marks that show paragraph endings and section breaks. Push the button again and you can't see them. For now, we want to see them, so push it again.

Would you like a line between columns? Go to the **Format** menu, then **Columns,** then click the box next to **Line between**.

Let's make a headline for our document. Place your cursor at the beginning, and type something like "My Newsletter," and hit **enter**.

```
My·Newsletter·¶
·xxx·xxx·xxxxx·xxxxx·x·xxxxxxxx·xxx·
xxx.·:··xxx·xxx·xxxxx·xxxxx·x·
xxxxxxxx·xxx·xxx.·:··xxx·xxx·xxxxx·
```

Now place your cursor right after My Newsletter, and **insert** another **continuous section break**.

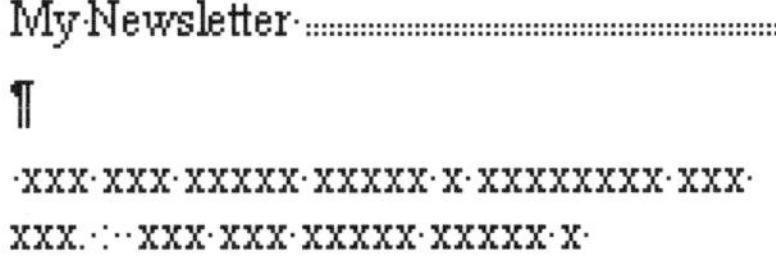

```
My·Newsletter·::::::::::::::::::::::::::::::::::::::
¶
·xxx·xxx·xxxxx·xxxxx·x·xxxxxxxx·xxx·
xxx.·:··xxx·xxx·xxxxx·xxxxx·x·
```

Now you need to highlight My Newsletter and change the font. How about making it 20 points and using center alignment? On my computer, I have to push the undo button each time I change the font or alignment, because the computer does the whole document, not just the section I am targeting. One push of the Undo button undoes the extra work.

Now, My Newsletter is aligned in the center and is in a separate little section of its own.

My·Newsletter·

¶

·xxx·xxx·xxxxx·xxxxx·x·xxxxxxxx·xxx·
xxx.·:··xxx·xxx·xxxxx·xxxxx·x·

Let's highlight My Newsletter again and make it one column, so it goes all across the top of the page. Find the column icon again, click it, and choose one column.

My·Newsletter·::::::Section Break (Continuous)::::::

·xxx·xxx·xxxxx·xxxxx·x·xxxxxxxx·xxx·
xxx.·:··xxx·xxx·xxxxx·xxxxx·x·
xxxxxxxx·xxx·xxx.·:··xxx·xxx·xxxxx·
xxx.·:··xxx·xxx·xxxxx·xxxxx·x·
xxxxxxxx·xxx·xxx.·:··xxx·xxx·xxxxx·
xxxxx·x·xxxxxxxx·xxx·xxx.·:··xxx·xxx·

Now, let's make some little headlines for the articles in the newsletter. In the body of the newsletter, after the first few "words," hit **enter.** This puts a paragraph mark after the words. They will be our small headline. Now, highlight them. Change the font size and align them to the center. (Remember to hit the undo button if the whole document changes, not just the headline.) Since these are part of the same section as the two columns, they will be in two-column format and will be just one column wide.

My·Newsletter·::::::Section Break (Continuous)::::::

xxx·xxx·xxxxx·xxxxx¶

·x·xxxxxxxx·xxx·xxx.·:··xxx·xxx·xxxxx·
xxxxx·x·xxxxxxxx·xxx·xxx.·:··xxx·xxx·
xxxxx·xxxxx·x·xxxxxxxx·xxx·xxx.·:··
xxxxxxxx·xxx·xxx.·:··xxx·xxx·xxxxx·
xxxxx·x·xxxxxxxx·xxx·xxx.·:··xxx·xxx·
xxxxx·xxxxx·x·xxxxxxxx·xxx·xxx.·:··
xxx·xxx·xxxxx·xxxxx·x·xxxxxxxx·xxx·
xxx.·:··xxx·xxx·xxxxx·xxxxx·x·

Add some more small headlines farther down, by separating them off using the **enter** key and following the same steps.

xxxxx·xxxxx·x·xxxxxxxx·xxx·xxx.·:··
xxx·xxx·xxxxx·xxxxx·x·xxxxxxxx·xxx·
xxx.·:··xxx·xxx·xxxxx·xxxxx·x·¶

xxxxxxxx·xxx·xxx¶

xxx·xxx·xxxxx·xxxxx·x·xxxxxxxx·xxx·
xxx.·:··xxx·xxx·xxxxx·xxxxx·x·

To make a different format on the second page, insert a continuous section break at the end of the first page. Then highlight all the things on the second page, and go to the **Format** menu, then **columns,** then select a format for the next page (or use the columns icon). Using the menu, you can get columns of unequal widths.

To insert a picture, put your cursor at the insertion point you want. Then go to the **Insert** menu, then picture, then choose where you want the picture to come from. It should come into your document in the proper size for the columns. But if it doesn't, click on it once to show the "handles" (little boxes around the rim). Click on a handle, hold the mouse button down, and move the handle around. You will find you can stretch the picture if you grab a handle on the top or side, while you re-size the picture proportionately if you grab a handle on a corner and move it inward or outward.

More on your word processor

Let's learn more about your word processor. Using trial and error, and the Help function, try using these menus:

- FILE – document access, input and output.
- EDIT – making document changes and word searches.
- VIEW – turning tools on and off such as toolbars, rulers, format views, header & footer.
- INSERT – introducing pictures, files, tables, page #, date.
- FORMAT – changing the look of your document, such as margins, fonts, and paragraph formats.
- TOOLS – spelling, grammar, and language tools as well as some more fancy stuff.
- TABLE – for drawing and editing text tables.
- WINDOW – managing multi windows or documents. This allows you to go back and forth between two open documents.
- HELP – accessing help tools previously discussed.

When you are using these major menus, you may find that not all the items in them are easily seen. Look for two down-pointing arrows at the bottom. Click on this symbol, and all the rest of the items show up.

Now, let's find a variety of templates (formatted letters, lists, memos, etc., for you to change and use). Look under File, then New. Open one of the template documents, such as a business letter, and save it under a new name. Then change it to meet your needs.

Exercise:

Using MS Word, format a page of any text as a newsletter with two or three columns.

Make a banner headline for the top of the newsletter. Create three articles with headlines, and a vertical line between columns. Make a second page with columns of unequal widths. Insert a picture and size it appropriately.

#9 A Spreadsheet

A spreadsheet is a computer program used to organize information for easy access and manipulation. The program also provides tools for graphing the data and performing math operations on the data. For you, the student, a spreadsheet might be useful for making a graph for a science project, or making a list of how you spent your money this month, providing an automatic way to add it all up.

Open your spreadsheet program. Ours is Microsoft Excel. Yours will probably be similar to that if not the same thing. In front of you, you see a sheet with *columns* (going up and down, like columns holding up a porch) and *rows* (going sideways). Have trouble remembering which is which? Think of rows in a theater; they go sideways.

The little rectangles that make up the columns and rows are called cells.

In Excel, the columns are labeled using the alphabet. The rows are labeled using numbers.

The columns contain data of the same type. That means the information you put in a column must be of the same kind, such as numbers, dollar amounts, or months of the year.

Rows contain data that are somehow related.

To get the idea, let's sort some blocks. We have three shades of gray. We have four types: circles, squares, rectangles, and ovals. How can we sort them into columns where the blocks are of the same type?

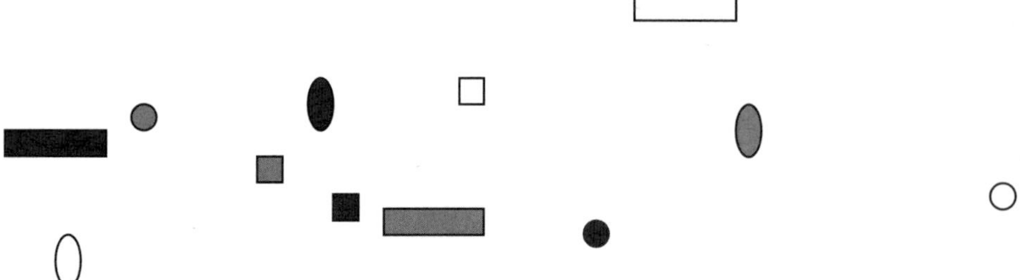

I'd like you to draw your result first and then look at mine.

Let's make our columns, where the items are the same type, based on the shape such as circle or square. How's this?

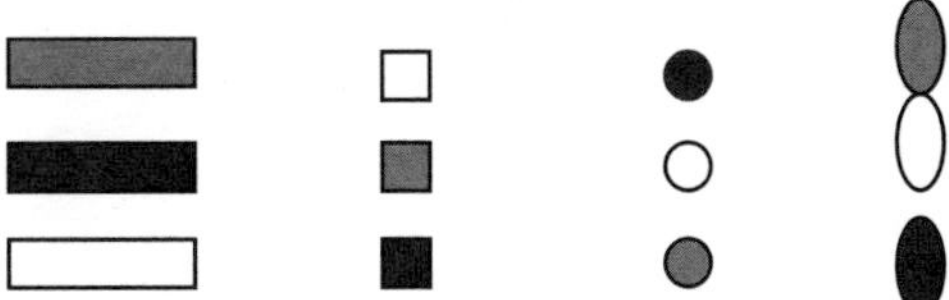

Well, we have everything in columns that are the same shape. But our rows don't contain related items. How else can we relate our items? By shade, of course. Our rows can be based on shade.

Our final result looks like this:

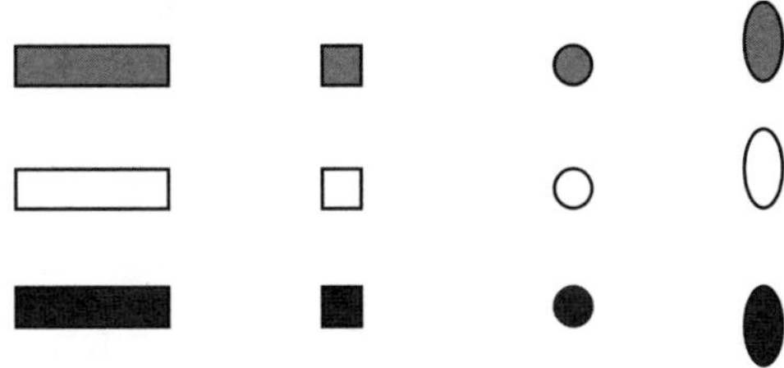

This is the sort of arrangement we need for a spreadsheet.

Now, let's take some information like name, age, weight, and height of two individuals we know:

Gianna 42 lb 50 inches

40 inches Lauren 30 lb

How would you organize it, with columns the same type of information, and rows somehow related? Jot down your answer and then turn the page.

Here's our result:

Gianna	42 lb	50 inches
Lauren	30 lb	40 inches

Now, we could give our columns labels so we all know what they are:

Name	weight	height
Gianna	42 lb	50 inches
Lauren	30 lb	40 inches

Putting it into a spread sheet

Putting information into a spreadsheet is as easy as just typing it in. But you do need to be careful to organize your data into columns and rows.

Let's make a spreadsheet on the computer of information about your family members. We will begin with four columns: Name, Age, Weight, and Height.

Go ahead and open up Excel. In row 3, Column C, type Name. Now:

In Column C, type Name.

In Column D, type Age.

In Column E, type Weight.

In Column F, type Height.

	A	B	C	D	E	F
1						
2						
3			Name	Age	Weight	Height
4						
5						
6						

Now, go back and put your cursor over one of the names you entered. Notice in the line above "ABCDEF" that it has been assigned a cell number, such as C1 or C6. That is how we find the data in a spreadsheet, with this address.

Underneath Name, Age, Weight and Height, fill in the data for several people. (You can make them up if you like.) Use height in inches or centimeters. You can use the arrow keys on your keyboard to move around a spreadsheet.

	A	B	C	D	E	F
1						
2						
3			Name	Age	Weight	Height
4			Hannah	15	110	64
5			Nathan	10	74	49
6			Samuel	10	85	48
7			Paul	10	74	47
8						

Now that we have the data entered, let's make a chart. Highlight only the squares you have filled in. Now click on the chart wizard icon:

Now we need to choose the chart type from this menu:

Let's choose column, the one at the top. We see a bunch of options on the left side for types of column graphs. Pick one.

Click "next." The computer shows you a bar graph with the data.

You can change the format of the graph by clicking "row" or "column" here.

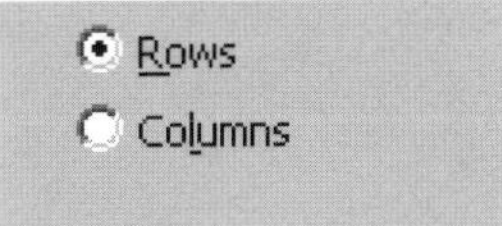

Let's click "rows."

Click "next" again. Fill in titles for the chart, the x axis (along the bottom edge) and the z axis (along the left edge).

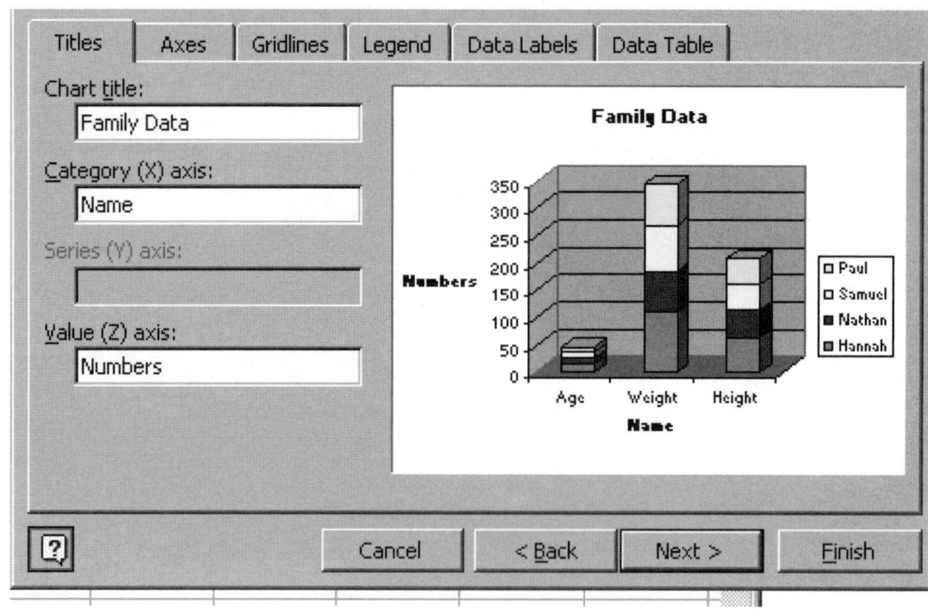

Now, click next, then finish. You have a bar graph!

You can make a bar graph for a science project easily this way. Try one using this data:

Chart title: Comparing growth in plant types

Plant type	Amount of Growth
Grass	0.5 inches
Corn	0.3 inches
Peas	0.4 inches

Remember what to do first? Input the data in columns and rows. Highlight the data. Click the chart wizard. Click the type of chart you want. Fill in title, x axis, z axis. Keep clicking "next" until you are done.

Now, let's make a pie chart. Let's put in some data about how much money the people in your family spent last week (as an example). Here is a sample you could use:

Hannah	7
Nathan	3
Sam	3
Paul	4

This becomes:

Name	Amount
Hannah	7
Nathan	3
Sam	3
Paul	4

We'd like the computer to know that the amounts are actually money. So click the column letter at the head of the column, and then find the icon for money, which looks like this: $. Click it. Presto, we have dollar signs!

Now, highlight the data, and click the chart wizard. Select pie chart as your chart type.

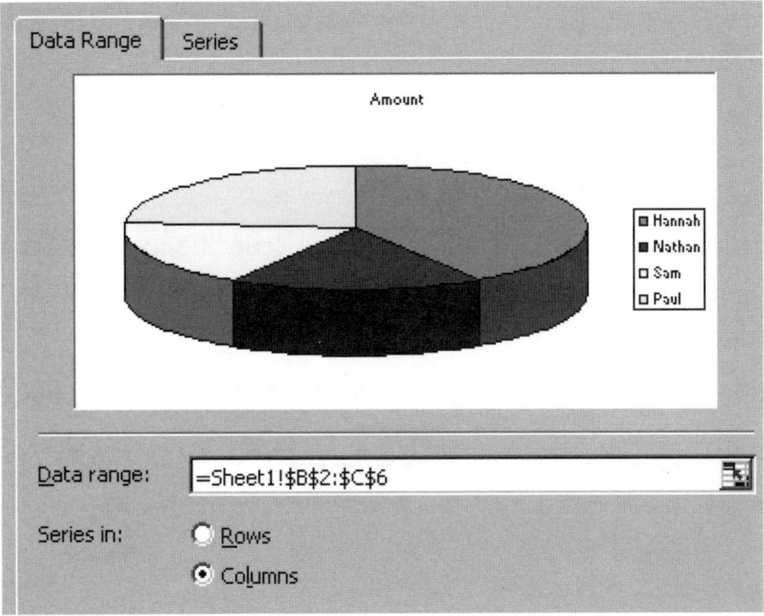

and go through the sequence again. If you don't like your result, click "back" or "cancel" and try something different. If you want to print it, highlight the chart and go to the file menu, and select print.

Save your sample so you can use it in the next lesson.

#10 More on Spread Sheets

Adding things up simply with a spread sheet

One of the most useful things about a spreadsheet is that it allows you to perform math operations on columns or rows of data. For example, let's say you wanted to find out the total weight in pounds of your family. You would use the "sum" function.

Open your spreadsheet.

Highlight all the numbers you entered in a column. Do not include the title.

Find the sum icon on the toolbar: Σ This is the Greek letter sigma, or S, for sum.

Click on the icon, and it automatically adds all the numbers you highlighted, and puts the sum in the next slot down in the column.

Now click on the cell with the sum in it. At the top you will see the addresses (range) of the cells being added.

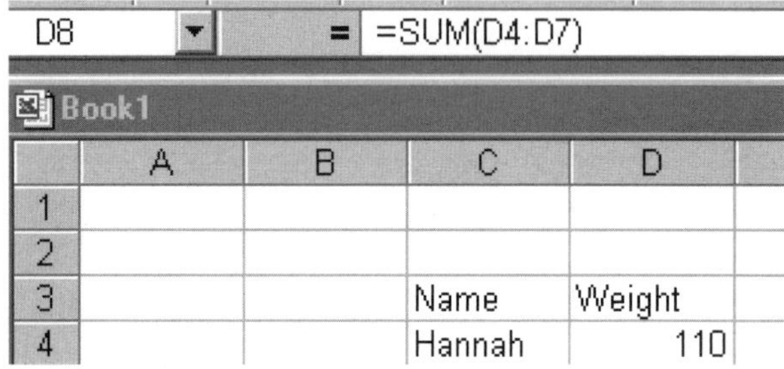

It's telling us at the top that cell D8 hold the sum of cells D4 through D7.

The average function

Let's create a new column to demonstrate the average function. Let's choose a column, say F, and write "Age" in Row 3.

Below that, fill in the ages of your family members, corresponding to the row containing their names.

Select the first blank cell at the bottom of the age column.

Click the **Insert** menu, then **function**, then **statistical,** then **average**. (Or, there is also an icon that looks like this: f_x that allows us to insert a function and choose which one.)

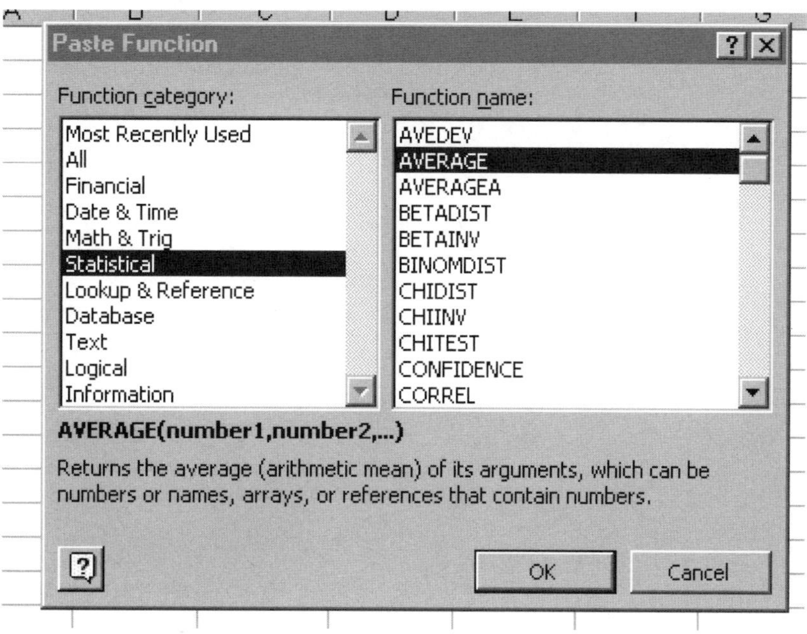

Click OK. Then you OK a listing of what cells you are averaging (based on what you had highlighted).

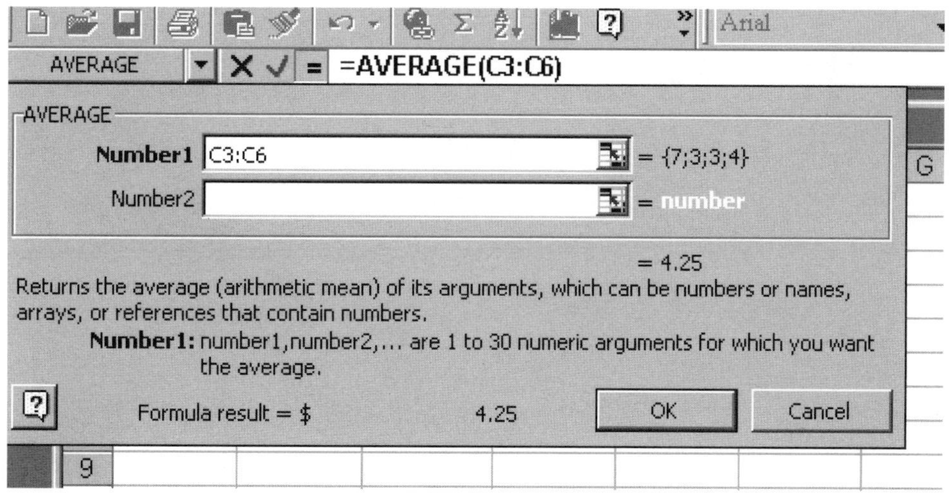

Click OK, and we're done!

Do you want your spreadsheet to look nice? Highlight all the cells you typed in, and then click on the **Format** menu, then **autoformat**, and then pick a format you like. Presto, it looks nice! More things to experiment with:

- Enter a date in a cell. Excel recognizes the format.
- Insert or delete columns and rows by selecting the column letter or row number, then going to the insert menu or pushing the delete button on your keyboard.
- Shade a column or row by selecting its letter or number, then clicking on the fill bucket icon.

Exercise:

Make a pie chart of living expenses for the year using Microsoft Excel. Use these numbers:

Food $2000

Shelter $2000

Clothing $500

#11 Internet Basics

Let's say you have a school assignment to learn about skyscrapers—how they are made, examples, and so on. You want to go to the Internet to find this information. Where do you start?

The Internet is like a whole lot of billboards. You the user can look at lots and lots of them. The people who put up the billboards have some costs that they have to cover somehow. They may also have a variety of reasons for posting their billboards. In order to evaluate what is on the billboard, you the user have to figure out why the owner of the billboard put it up and how he or she is paying for it. Once you figure out why the owner put the billboard up, you will know whether to trust what the billboard is saying. We need to figure this out because there is plenty of information on the Internet that is misleading.

Let's go to www.google.com, a "search engine" that helps us search, and type into the search window some key words. For our skyscraper project, let's type in **skyscraper kids construction**. We are choosing these key words because we want to know about skyscraper construction, but we don't want a lot of technical specifications. The word "kids" should make sure the material is easy to understand.

The Google search engine digs up a whole lot of Web sites that contain our key words. It puts some sites higher up on the list than others based on criteria that include how often the key words occur in the page, and whether the site gets a lot of hits. So you the user can expect to see a list of Web sites that will be helpful to you.

Look at the list Google has generated for you. We want to learn to evaluate various sites on this list without actually going to them, in order to become speedy users of the Internet, going to just the right site quickly. Each listing has several lines and, near the bottom, the URL (universal resource locator) address. This looks like this: www.mysite.com, or something similar.

How to find the right info

As it happens, we want some information. We don't want to buy a book or a video or anything else. We want to find a Web site where someone has gone to the expense to post useful information that we can access for free. There should be some of these out there, believe it or not.

Many Web sites have a commercial basis, meaning they intend to turn a profit. This is the .com part of the URL address. Other possibilities are .net, for network, .org for nonprofit organization, .edu for educational institution, and two-letter abbreviations for various countries, such as .uk for United Kingdom, and .ca for Canada.

On our Google list of Web sites, we can see some .com sites that mention the word "book" or "video." We can assume that these sites are selling books and are not handing out free information.

There is one from www.pbs.org. We know how this site is probably paid for—using the same sources of funding that PBS television specials use. This is a very likely place to look for good free information. Let's click on this listing to go to the Web site. When we get there, find the link near the top of the page that says "home" and click on that, to be sure we are at the main home page for the PBS Building Big Web site. Go down to the bottom of the page. This is normally where we can find the information about who put the Web site up. Here, it tells us that the public TV station in Boston, WGBH, put up the site, and it lists sponsors. Can we trust skyscraper information from this site? I would.

Now, go back to Google's search page and type in "Daniel Boone." Let's look for free information on this pioneer.

Google shows us a list. Look at one that has the URL www.berksweb.com. Does the URL tell us anything? It sounds like it might be the personal Web site of a person named Berks. If that were the case, we would have to take what it says with a grain of salt. But a little higher up in the listing, it mentions Berks County, Pa. This must be the Web site for that county. Its purpose is probably to provide information. We can probably trust what it says.

Some of the others are obviously selling books, we can tell from the listing.

Here's an odd one: www.lucidcafe.com. What could that be? Let's check it out. It shows a biography page on Daniel Boone. Scroll down to the bottom. It should indicate where the page came from. Well, sure enough it does, sort of—there is a click-on ad for coffee! What is going on? Go up a little farther and we see we can buy books and videos on Daniel Boone.

Let's go to the top of the page now and click on Lucidcafe home. We find that Lucidcafe is selling coffee, books and art. So, here's the answer—it's like a big bookstore with a coffee shop, only in cyberspace. They let you browse for free in their biography section, including one on Daniel Boone. Now that we see what they are up to, we can decide whether to trust what they say.

Here are the things we need to consider when deciding whether to trust a Web site:

- Who is paying for the Web site and why?
- What is the author's expertise on the subject? Can you figure out from the Web site whether the author has credentials?
- Take a look at the date the Web page was last updated. Was it five years ago? If so it may be no longer accurate.
- Even if you are looking at a site from a source you trust, you may find links there to other sites that are not so trustworthy.

Let's say we want to use the information we found on lucidcafe.com on Daniel Boone. What is the best way? Information in books or on the Internet is copyrighted. That means that it belongs to the owner, and we can only copy it with permission from the owner.

To run off a legal copy for most Web pages, we can go to the file menu and print, or press the print icon. This will give us a copy of the page, complete with ads probably, that is legally sanctioned by the owner of the site, with the URL printed at the bottom.

We can quote small pieces of it in a paper we might be writing, but we need to tell our readers where the information came from. To do this, highlight a paragraph, then go to the edit menu, and click on copy. Now shrink down the browser window, and open your word processor. Use edit, then paste to paste the paragraph into the Word processor file. Now go back to the Web site and copy information from it about whose site it is, and also the URL, and paste those into your word processor file too. Also record the date you accessed the Web site; Web sites change over time, and someone reading your paper later and wanting to find the information might find it gone. All this is the type of information you would put in a footnote or at the end of the paper in a bibliography.

On "Borrowing"

When we get around to making a Web site of our own, we have to be wary of "borrowing" information from other Web sites without getting permission from the owner to use it. We could "borrow" all kinds of animations, music, and information from around the Web, but we would be violating copyright law! This takes money out of the pocket of the person who created the stuff we are "borrowing." Would you want someone to do that to you? Don't do it to them. Also, be warned that there are cases like this being prosecuted in the courts. They are even suing teenagers!

While we're on the subject of illegal things, let's talk about hacking. Hackers are generally young computer-savvy folks who want to cause a little mischief. So they create little programs that do damage; these are called viruses. They package the viruses in email attachments and, rarely, on Web sites. They also might cross the Internet to burrow into a computer server to get information they want, getting around the password requirements and so on. Sometimes they can get information that they are not entitled to have, including bank account numbers.

Please be warned that this may look like mischief to the hacker, but what is really going on is big trouble for both the hacker and the victim. Victims have suffered millions of dollars worth of damages to their systems, and their pocketbooks, and hackers have gone to jail for a while. So don't do that either.

Useful skills

Something else we might want to do while on the Internet is store an address so we can go back to it later. This is called "bookmarking" or "favorites." First, go to the page you are interested in. Then find the **Bookmark** or **Favorites** menu at the top of the page of the browser. Click on it, then on **Add to Favorites**. This will put your bookmark in a list of favorites. To arrange the list and put related items in the same folder, choose **Favorites**, then **Organize Favorites**.

Let's learn a useful skill: finding driving directions, including distances between one point and another. In the blank line near the top of the browser window, type in www.mapquest.com. This pulls up a Web site that will provide a map for you. What we want is a map from one place to another, so we click on the round icon near the middle of the top that says "Driving Directions." Once there, you enter addresses for the place you start and for the place you end up (your destination). Click on "Get Directions." You will see a list of directions that tells the driver where to turn, and then how far to drive before the next turn. This is the "fastest route." If you don't like it, try the "shortest route," from the tab button just above the directions. Or the route that avoids highways.

If you scroll down the page you will see some maps of your beginning and end points. You can make the maps zoom in and out by clicking on the zoom scale, or pan sideways by clicking the edge of the map where you want the "camera" to move.

Let's say you like the route you have found and want to print it out. You can pull up a printer-friendly version, which doesn't use up lots of colored ink on ads. To do this, click on "print route." Once you have the printer-friendly version, you can print it by choosing the **File** menu and then **Print**, or you can hit **control-P**.

What if you don't know an exact address in the city of interest, but you want a map that includes the city? At the top of the page, click on the round icon that says Maps. There is a place to enter an address, and above it some links including one that says "Airport." Click on this and choose the airport of the city you want. Then you can use the map zoom and pan buttons to look over the city, state, or country.

Weather reports

What if you are wondering what the weather report is, in your city or in some other city? You could pretend you are going on a trip to a faraway state and are wondering what the weather will be like so you will know what clothes to pack.

Type this URL into the white space near the top: www.weather.com. When it comes up, you will find a blank space near the top of the page that says "Enter city or U.S. zip code." Enter the zip code or city, and click on "Go." Near the top is the near-term weather forecast. Go down farther to find a radar map showing clouds and other weather in the area. Go even further down for a 10-day forecast.

Let's take a good look at the map. Find the legend at the top that shows what colors indicate what kinds of precipitation. You can enlarge the map by clicking on it, and then animate the radar images by clicking on a link below the map that says, "Map in Motion." This shows several recent still images of the local radar taken every 15 minutes.

To see the big weather picture in the U.S., hit the "back" arrow on the upper left of your screen to go back to the previous screen, or put www.weather.com back in the top white space. Down a little ways you see a U.S. map. Click on it to enlarge and examine it, and on a nearby button to animate it.

Remember that any information on the Internet is dated. That is, it was posted at a particular time, and that may be a few weeks ago or a day ago. So the map might not show the latest construction project, and the weather report might not be updated over the weekend.

12 Web Design: Getting Started

Now that I am used to using the Internet a little, I can ask, what is happening when I "browse"?

When you go to a web page, your computer, using its *browser* (an application such as Internet Explorer or Netscape Navigator), has gone out over the phone lines and pulled some code from a storage computer, called a *server.* Your browser uses this code to construct what you are looking at.

Let's see what the code is. At the top of the browser screen is a list of menus. Find the one that says **View.** Put your mouse arrow on it. Various options in the **View** menu appear. Click on the one that says **Source** or **Page source.**

A window pops up to show you the source code for the Web site. You see lines of text and a lot of hypertext tags (words enclosed like <this>). The tags are special code that tells your browser how to display the rest of the text. When you look at the Web page normally, the tags don't show. In a way, the source code is like the procedures page in MicroWorlds, which lists all the instructions, and the browser page is like the drawing page in MicroWorlds, which shows the result.

The tags also tell the browser to pull in information from other files, such as picture files or "links" to related Web pages.

Let's Get Organized

We are going to construct a simple Web page in this tag language, which is called **HTML** for hypertext markup language. The first thing we have to think about is where we are going to call our pictures (image files) from, and how we will link our pages together. We have to set up a file system that will do the job, on paper at first. As we create the real files, we will name them and link them so that they fit together like pieces in a puzzle!

I will assume that you have at least two people making Web pages, or one person making at least two pages. We will have each page created in a folder which will contain the master HTML file for the page, and also the pictures that it draws on. We will also need a home page, which by Internet convention should be named "**index**." "Index" will be in a folder of its own as well, containing the pictures it calls. All the folders will be stored in a master folder.

Now, let's create those folders. Click the "**my computer**" icon on your PC desktop:

Now click on the C: drive (your hard drive).

Near the top of the window you will see the File menu. 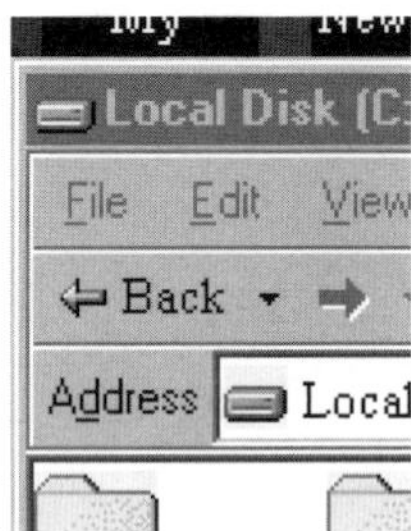

Click on **File**, then on **new**, then **folder**. A new folder will appear in the window with the name "new folder." Use the right mouse button to click on the folder. Some options appear; select "**rename**." Rename it "**master**." This folder's name is now **C:\master**. (You can capitalize these names or not. The computer doesn't distinguish capital letters for these file names.)

Now, click on the master folder. Again click on file, new, folder. This creates a folder inside "master." Rename this new folder as **yourname**. This will hold your Web page. If you are doing two Web pages, click on the master folder again, file, new, folder, and rename it as **yourname1.** Do the same for anyone else who is creating a Web page alongside you. Be sure you use just these names, since the files have to call each other, and computers require everything to match perfectly. Each web page folder's name is now **C:\master\yourname** or **C:\master\yourname1**. But now that we are dealing with HTML, we will switch the way the slashes go. They are **C:/master/yourname** and **C:/master/yourname1.** The computer reads them the same, whether the slashes go forward or backward.

Make another Web page folder for the home page. Click on the master folder, then click file, new, folder. We have a third folder inside of master. Name it **index.** Its name is now **C:/master/index.** Your setup should look like this:

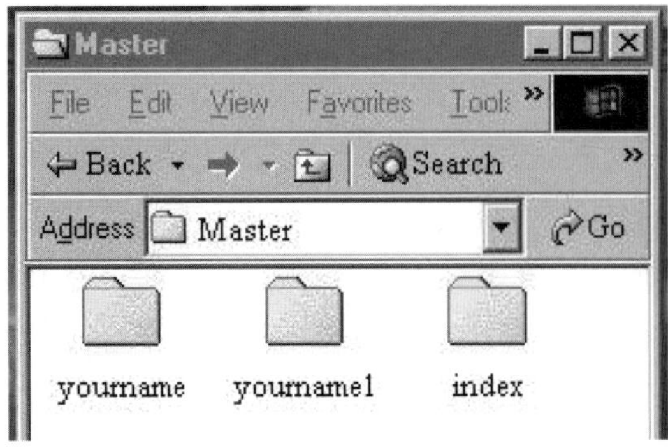

Find a Topic

What to make a Web page about? You have a lot of leeway here, obviously. You will need to gather a bunch of information on a topic and write it down, rather like writing a paper. Then you need to format it for the Internet. Since we have already done some work on drawing skyscrapers, our class wrote a Web page about skyscrapers. That way we could post the buildings we drew as illustrations. (Or you can choose a different topic and get different illustrations.) Look in the Appendix for ideas.

Get Graphics Files: .gif and .jpeg

Computer illustrations are called graphics or images. You can recognize the ones your browser can use because their file names end with **.gif** or **.jpeg**. You can get them from:

- drawings or photos that have been scanned (made into digital files)
- pictures from a digital camera
- drawings made by some computer programs, including MicroWorlds
- the Internet.

Try to use illustrations that have low resolution, or few pixels per inch. (A really low resolution will make your picture blurry.) Lower-resolution pictures will download to a user's browser more quickly. You can control resolution, if you are using a scanner, before you run the final scan, or on a digital camera, before you take the picture. Seventy-two pixels per inch works pretty well for most Internet illustrations.

Remember, if you use any writing or images that you did not create, you need to have permission to publish it on the Internet. You can download images from the Internet, but make sure the page they come from says they are free, or else get permission from the site owner. You can pick up nearly any image on the Internet by right-clicking it, and from the menu that appears choose "copy" or "save as." Then save it into one of your Web site folders.

Drag and Drop Using Two Windows

Now, let's put your available graphics in the file **yourname.** You can use a drag-and-drop method to do that. Let's say the file you want came from a scanner or a digital camera. It is on a floppy disk. Go to the "my computer" icon on your desktop. Click on it. You will see the A: drive and the C: drive. First, click on the C: drive, then click on **Master**, then on **Yourname**. Now shrink this **Yourname** window down using the half-size window-shrink button in the upper right corner next to the x. Now move the window off to the right by grabbing its blue "handle" on top and moving your mouse to the side, then letting up on the mouse button.

Now click again on the my-computer icon, **A:** drive this time, and shrink the box to half size. Put the boxes next to each other. (Remember how to do this trick. We will use it more.)

Now you can "drag and drop" items from the **A:** window to the **Yourname** window. When you do this, the computer moves the file into the new place. In my illustration, I want to move a picture file called areodactyl to my Yourname folder. To make sure you leave a copy behind on the A: drive, you can first highlight the file in the A: window, then click on edit, then copy. Move the cursor over to the destination window, click there, and click on edit, then paste. (If you drag and drop, you may find your original copy has moved to the new file.)

Let's make an image of the building you drew in MicroWorlds. Open MicroWorlds and pull up your building file. Run the command to draw the building. (Or, draw another building using the tools in the paintbrush icon.) Color it in if you like, using the paint buckets. In the command center, hide the turtle by running the command **ht**. Then run this command: **savehtml "c:\master\yourname.**

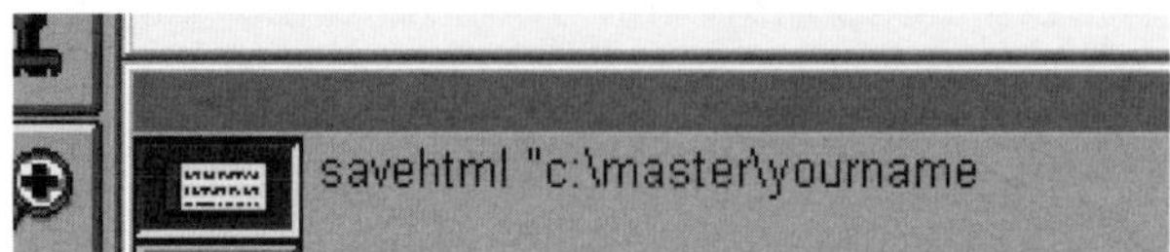

This will put a **.gif** file that pictures your building in the folder yourname. It will also put in an HTML file that you don't need. It automatically names them both *page1*.

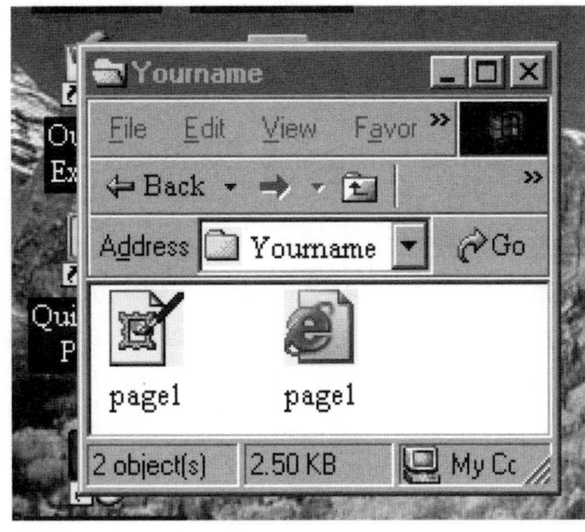

Delete the HTML file – the one that has the browser icon, in my case a large e for Internet Explorer. This leaves page1.gif, your picture file.

Next, you need to gather information on skyscrapers, or whatever your topic is. (To see questions we answered, see the appendix.) Write a paragraph of at least eight sentences in your word processor on it. Make sure there are absolutely no spelling or grammar errors. (These are much harder to fix later.) Run the spell-checker, and also have an adult look it over. Put a headline at the top.

Create Your HTML File

You will need to open up a simple word processor on your computer called Wordpad (or Notepad), which can save your text in HTML format. Here's how you open Wordpad. At the bottom left of your screen is a Start button. Click on that that. Click on programs, then accessories, then Wordpad. Now from the file menu, choose open, and open your document. (If Wordpad can't open it, you will need to open it in the regular word processor and **copy** the text, then open Wordpad and **paste** it into the file there.)

Now we need to transform our Wordpad file into an HTML file, with a .html extension. Click on file, save, and select the location you need: C:\master\yourname. Look at the bottom of the box that shows up. Change the type of file to **text**. Type in the entire new name of this file, including the extension (yourname.html). Click save. You'll get an error message wondering if you want to get rid of all formatting in saving as a text file. Say OK, or format as text. Now you have an HTML file!! If you don't, find the file icon, right-click on it, and rename it as yourname.html.

Note: When you want to close this file and then re-open it to edit it, you will need to open up Wordpad or Notepad first, and use the File-Open menus to get to your file. Then when you save it, make sure that the title of the file contains the .html extension. If you are going back and forth between Wordpad and your browser, it would be a good idea to shrink them down rather than close them. When you make changes in Wordpad and save them, you need to go to the browser page and push the **refresh** button to see the changes. Or you could close the browser and then go to the My Computer icon, and keep opening folders till you get to your folder. Then you could click on the icon for your html file that matches your browser. This will open up the file using the browser with the latest version.

#13 Web Design: Let's Code

Our HTML file contains the text we want to display, but it contains no tag commands to the browser on how to display it. We need to add these commands. These tags generally come in pairs: at the beginning of our file goes the tag <html>, to open the html interpreter, and at the very end </html>, to turn it off. At the beginning of the heading comes <head>, and at the end of the heading is </head>. At the beginning of a paragraph, <p>. After the paragraph, </p>. And so on. It's not hard!

At the very top of the page, type this: <html>

Now, at the end of the file, after your text, type this:: </html>

Our HTML file will have two sections: the header and the body. The body is the part that shows in the Web page. The header is information that appears in indexes and in the very top line about the page title.

So let's fill in lines before and after our text like this:

```
<html>
<head>
</head>
<body>
Your headline and article go here
</body>
</html>
```

Now we will add the title in the header.

```
<html>
<head>
<title>
Put in a title for  the tippy top of page, in blue band, such as My Web Page
</title>
</head>
<body>
Your headline and article go here
</body>
</html>
```

Inside the body, let's put paragraph marks in, <p> at the beginning of each paragraph, and </p> at the end.

The tags should be nested. That is, inside the outer pair of tags of <html> and </html> are some inner pairs, such as <body> and </body>. Between the <body> and </body> tags we might find more tag pairs, such as <p> and </p>. But we can't put a <p> tag before <body> and the corresponding </p> tag after </body>.

When you save your Wordpad/Notepad file, use Save rather than Save As, and type in the .html extension to the file name. You have to click on the type of file to change the way it will save, and save it as a text file. If you are using Notepad, you will need to type the .html file extension every time you save.

Let's take a look at it!

Shrink down your Wordpad window to half size. Now open your file using your browser. Here's how: on your desktop, click on the My Computer icon, then C:, then Master, then Yourname, then the html icon (e or a net) for the file Yourname. (If the icon for your file doesn't look like an e for explorer or a net for Netscape, you have not managed to save it as an html file! Try again.)

How does it look?

If it doesn't display, your code needs some adjustments. You've forgotten one of the tags or slash marks or made some other tiny error. Enlarge Wordpad/Notepad again make the changes. Carefully go over your file, looking for pairs of tags, one to open and one to close. Look for more troubleshooting suggestions in the HTML section of the Appendix. Save the file again as HTML, shrink Wordpad, and enlarge the browser again. You can hit the refresh button (it looks like a rectangle with arrows going in circles on it) or re-open the file. When you do get the file to display, it should look like a bunch of text, with "My Web Page" in the blue band at the top.

We are switching back and forth between a Wordpad window and a browser window. Here's a big difference from MicroWorlds. With this setup, changes we make on our Wordpad "procedures page" don't automatically show up in our browser display, unless we save the file with changes and then refresh the code the browser is seeing.

We can make adjustments to the tags. Instead of just **<title>** for an opening title tag, try this:

> **<Title Align=center>** (or you could say align=left or right).

Make your headline stand out.

> **<h1> <center> This makes a centered headline in the biggest of font sizes, h1. You can also use h2 , h3, on to h6, the smallest. </h1>**

Some paragraph formats:

> **<p> This command gives us a new paragraph. </p>**
>
> **<p> <i> This gives us a new paragraph, in italic. </i> </p>**
>
> **<p> <b> This gives us a new paragraph, in bold type. </b> </p>**
>
> **
 Put this in where you want to start a new line. It's called a line break.**

Don't forget these closing tags:

> **</body>**
>
> **</html>**

Let's change the background color. Find the first body tag. Make it look like this:

> **<body bgcolor="#ff0000">.**

This makes it red. For blue, use #0000ff. For green, #008000. For purple, #800080.

Another way to make a new paragraph is to add a line break, which is the equivalent of pressing the "enter" button to make a new paragraph. This is a **
** tag. There is no closing tag for it; it stands alone.

Pictures

Let's insert your picture. To put it along the left side of the text, let's put in a tag that is after the first paragraph tag, **<p>,** but before the first text.

```
<p><img src="page1.gif"> Put some text here...</p>
```

The "src" refers to "source." We're telling the browser to look alongside this file, in the same file folder, for the image, which is saved as page1.gif.

Want to center the image? Don't put it in the same paragraph with the text. Make that

```
<center> <img src="page1.gif"></center>
<p> Put some text here ...</p>
```

Want a picture border of thickness 10 pixels? make that

```
<center> <img src="page1.gif" border=10></center>
```

Our image as it comes from MicroWorlds is pretty big. Want it re-sized? You can re-size it in a photo application, but maybe you don't have one. If not, you need to specify the size in pixels. This will take some trial and error, since we don't know how big it is to begin with. The new width and height should be in the same proportion as the old, in order to keep the image looking good. Try this:

```
<img src="page1.gif" width=300 height=200 >
```

If it looks odd, try something different.

Let's align the image to the right side of the page, and add some horizontal space:

```
<img src="page1.gif" width=300 height=200 align=right hspace=20>
```

This will give you an image 300 pixels wide, 200 tall, aligned to the right side of the page, and with 20 pixels of horizontal space added beside the image. (For vertical space, vspace.)

Save it and then reopen it with your browser. What do you think?

Relative Links

Let's insert a link to another Web page of ours. Our link (what the user will click on) needs to read "Go to Homepage." But what do we write in the part of the link that calls the file name? We can use a *relative* file name for this, not a full address or URL. Here's how we do it. We pretend to walk across our file organization map from one file to the other. First, let's look at the map.

Remember, we are currently in the folder **Yourname,** in the file *yourname.html.* We need to "walk" to *index.html* in the **index** folder. Our file organization map looks like this:

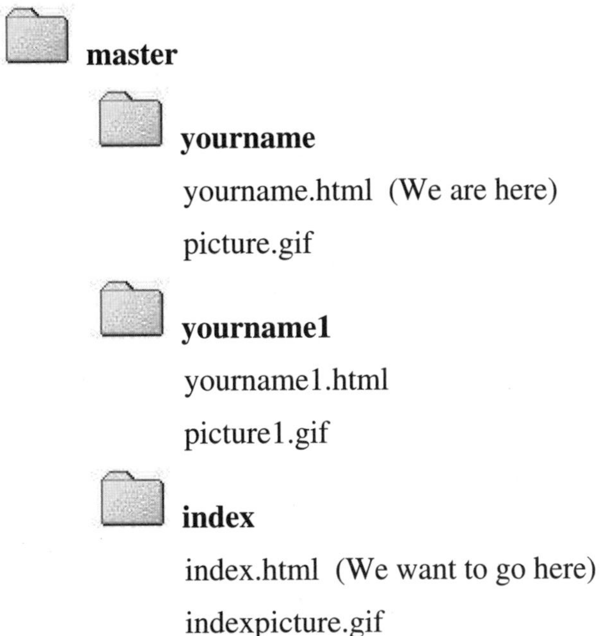

To get from where we are to where we want to go, we have to leave the folder **yourname** and go up a step into the street, so to speak. We need to go "up one level." The next-up folder's *relative* address starts with "**../**" which means, "go up a level." Then we walk down the street, figuratively. From that level we need to step down into the **index** folder, and from there into the file *index.html.* So our path looks like this: **../index/index.html** and our link looks like this**:**

<a href="../index/index.html"> Go to Homepage </a>

Notice that the text the user will click on, "Go to Homepage," is enclosed in <a> tags.

You also want to put a link on the *index* page that will take the user to the page *yourname.* Can you think what that relative address will look like? "Standing" at *index.html*, you need to go up one level, out into the street, and down into the folder **yourname** to *yourname.html.* Your path will be **../yourname/yourname.html.**

It's considered normal Internet protocol to have links to all three of your pages on all three of the pages. So you can create a set of three links and use copy and paste to put this list on all your pages. Of course, the result is that each page links to the other two and also to itself.

Outside links

We also need to provide links to outside Web sites. For one of these, we need to type:

<a href="http://www.whateverthewebsite.com"> Name of Web Site that shows</a>

Something else we will need: a link to an email address. Type this:

<a href=mailto:name@site.com> Click here to e-mail a question</a>

Check that your links work by viewing your page from the browser and clicking on the link. The browser should be able to access pages you made if you have arranged your links and folders well. Outside links will show an error message, but will also tell you exactly what the browser was looking for, to allow you to check for errors. Or, if you are connected to the Internet, they should take you to the outside Web site.

About smart quotes

There are certain characters that Microsoft uses in Word and Power Point that are nonstandard and will not read properly in HTML. These include the "smart quotes" that curl around the word instead of hanging straight, as well as dashes. So if you create HTML code in Word, certain characters won't display properly. The fix is this: always copy your text from Word and paste it into Wordpad or Notepad, as I have suggested here. Wordpad and Notepad substitute standard characters automatically. Or create it from scratch in Wordpad or Notepad.

Uploading your site

Once your site is working—all the links work properly—you are ready to talk to your Internet provider about uploading it. You will upload the contents of your "**master**" folder. The provider will give you detailed instructions and a password to get your files onto its server. Depending on your provider, there can be a fee for hosting your Web site.

See the Appendix for a list of HTML commands and troubleshooting advice.

#14 Web Design: Using a Web Editor

Now that we have made a Web page using HTML code, we can take a short cut and still understand what we are doing. The shortcut is an application, a Web editor, that allows you to manipulate what the browser sees, while the application writes the code in the background. It would be like moving the MicroWorlds characters around on page1, and in doing so automatically creating code on the hidden procedures page.

First, have someone download a free application for you called Cool Page. It's at http://www.coolpage.com. (For information on how to download, see Logo Lesson 12.) Next, select a topic for your next Web site and collect information. Write a report of 10 to 20 sentences, in at least two paragraphs. Arrange for a photo or scanned drawing of your subject. Have that available on a disk.

Our group chose to add to the Web site for the church most of us attend. You could build a similar Web site for any group you belong to. We interviewed various adults in the church and asked them what they liked about the church, and asked them to describe church programs. We took photos of our subjects with a digital camera. Many of us also interviewed ourselves and took a picture, making a personal Web page too. All this took us a couple of weeks. (For more information, see Appendix I.)

Getting started with Cool Page:

Now that you are ready with content, open Cool Page.

Click the objects icon (a square with windows in it fairly near the top of the screen). Your page will be on the left, a list in the center, and a group of icons to choose from on the right.

From the central list, choose "background." A variety of backgrounds appears on the right. Drag one over to the page on the left. Or, go with a solid color; double-click on the background. A color toolbar appears. Choose a color.

Add text:

Shrink the Cool Page window.

I am assuming you have written your text in another application, such as Word. Open your document application and **copy** your text.

Close the document application.

Enlarge Cool Page.

Click a spot on the page. Under the edit menu, click **paste**. The text will make a text box as it comes in. To adjust the size of the text box, click on the box to select it. Drag the corners and handles to re-size.

To color the text, highlight it and then change the color in the little box near the font icons.

Add objects:

From the central list, click on animations. A list of animations appears on the right. Drag and drop some over to your page. Do the same with sounds, etc.

Create a filing system:

At this point we need to decide how we are organizing these Web page files. Let's say we are creating a home page called index, and two pages called yourname and yourname1. We will need three folders named index, yourname, and yourname1. Inside each is an html file of the same name, plus the other files that the Web site uses, such as **.gif** or **.jpeg** files. The three folders I mentioned are stored alongside each other in a larger folder, Mypage.

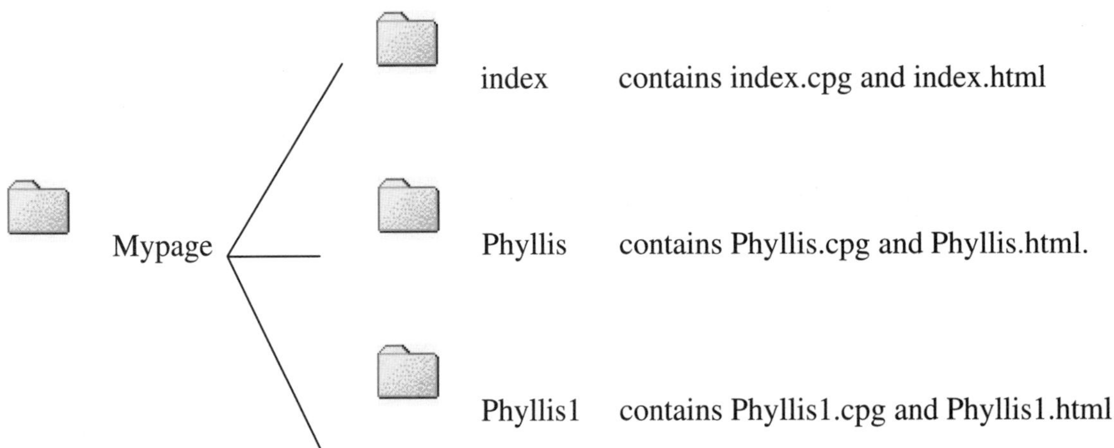

You can create these folders using the My Computer icon, clicking on file, then new, then folder. For now they will be empty—we will put the HTML files there when we are done.

Save in a temporary spot

The Cool Page application saves files in its own format, which we should do while we are still working on the files. (The format isn't usable by a browser.) From the Cool Page file menu, click on save as. You can create new folders from this menu, by clicking on the little folder with the asterisk next to it, at the right.

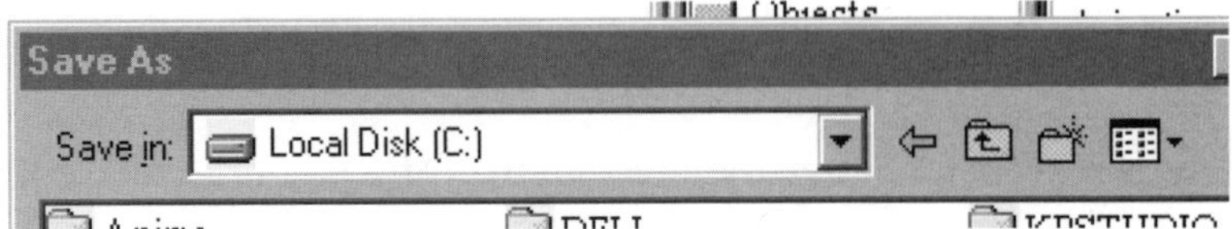

From Local Disk (C:), create a temporary file to hold the Cool Page files. Click on the new folder icon, then make folder called tempcoolpage, and put your Cool Page files in there.

Add objects you take from the Internet, or photos:

Cruise around on the Internet. You can pick up backgrounds, pictures, animation, or sounds.

Backgrounds: To look for a background, you can try www.freebackgrounds.com/plaza.htm or www.grsites.com/textures. Look out, though. Do not click on any other items on these pages. They will just take you somewhere where they will try to sell you something and waste your time! Remember that a busy background makes it difficult to read the text on your web page. Keep it simple and easy on the eyes.

For pictures, go to Google.com and type in **image subject free**, where you choose the subject. You want "free" files because you want images the photographer has decided to share for free. Look for files ending in .jpeg or .gif.

For animation, you could check www.animationlibrary.com/a-l/.

To look for a sound file, type in a composer or music type, then **midi** (the ending on a type of music file), then **free**. Google will lead you to lots of possibilities. Other file types you can use are MP3 and wav.

You can also record a sound or rhythm if you have a microphone, using the recording software in you "accessories" on your computer, alongside Wordpad. Beware, though, of loud or obnoxious sounds! You don't want to drive users away from your Web site!

On the Internet, when you find an animation, background, midi file, or anything you like, make sure that the page says it is free. Then save it this way: Put your cursor on top of the image you want to save. Right click on the mouse. A menu will open up, and you drag down to "Save As." Click on that. You can rename the image for easier finding as you put it on your floppy disk.

Now, open Cool Page and shrink it halfway (using the double shrink box icon in upper right). Move the whole window to the right and down by grabbing it by the blue band at the top and dragging it. Make it smaller by pushing inward from the lower right corner.

On the desktop, click on the "my computer" icon (or the computer name), and then click on A:. This is your floppy drive. You will get an A: window which you also want to shrink to half size and place next to the Cool Page box. Now, you can drag items from the A: window and drop them into the Cool Page Web page. Do this to add the objects you got off the Internet, and the photo. Save your Cool Page file.

View your page in HTML:

Click **preview**, an icon at the top right. This will prompt you to name your Web page. (This isn't the file name; it's the name that appears at the tippy top of the page when a browser displays it.) Name your page. You will also be asked for a description. Type in the first few lines of text that appear on your Web page, to allow a search engine to pinpoint exactly what is in it. You will need to click the preview icon again to see your page from your browser.

Add links:

Near the bottom of your page, create a text box and type the word "**Home**" in it. Now, highlight the text. Near the top right of the screen, there is a place to type in the link information that now becomes active. Type the URL in here:

http://www.yourwebsite/index/index.html

You will need three links on each page, following standard Web convention—each page even has a link to itself. Make these other links:

"**Interview with Karri**" (for example). Highlight it, then type this for the link:

http://www.yourwebsite/yourname/yourname.html

"**About me.**" Highlight it, then type in this for the link:

http://www.yourwebsite/yourname1/yourname1.html

Or, you can use the relative links we discussed before, with "../" standing for "go up a level."

As a licensing condition for using this free software, we are supposed to have a link to the Cool Page website on our page. This is a little icon that appears on your page when you first create it. Make sure the icon stays there!

Save your page as HTML:

When you are done with your page and ready to publish it, start from Cool Page, not the browser. Open your file. Click the **File** menu, then **export**. When the computer asks where to put it, click on C:\Mypage, then on the folder you have created with the same name as the file**: Index, yourname,** or **yourname1**. To upload it, follow directions from your Internet service provider.

Our Requirements

- An interview written in the third person. For jr. high, at least 8 sentences. For sr. high, at least 15 sentences. Use first names and last initials only.
- Absolutely no spelling or grammar errors.
- Appropriate content in all respects.
- (Optional: a personal Web page, "About Me." It is for extra credit only.)
- Background and at least three images—photos, animations, etc.
- Optional: mild appropriate sound. No loud or obnoxious noises.
- Links: On each page, "Home," "About Me" (if you have a personal page) and "Interview with Kari (or whoever)."
- At least one image or animation that you got from the Internet or a CD-ROM, not Cool Page.
- The Cool Page button placed at the bottom of your screen.

#15 Teach Yourself More Word Processing

Advanced formatting features

In order to create better-looking documents, there's a lot to learn about a word processor. Go back to your previous word processing lesson and refresh your memory about how to format a newsletter. Now, on your default page, type a few lines of anything. Highlight your text and then use the **help** function to look these up:

- Formatting a document
- Setting tabs
- Using bullets
- Changing margins
- Using multi columns
- Headers and footers
- Using Rulers
- Drawing objects
- Colors
- Tables
- Graphics
- Word art
- Format styles
- Envelopes and labels
- Macros

#16 Logo Variables

What if we want to draw a building, like before, but this time we want to be able to tell the computer to draw it twice as big? Or half as big? We will be able to do this once we figure out how to use *variables*. These are values, like the height of the building, that can vary, or change, but at the same time are represented with just one name. *Height* is an example of a variable name.

Let's talk variables

When you start a program, such as MicroWorlds or Word or Excel, you usually double click on an icon. This is an instruction to the operating system to look on the hard drive and find the program that is associated with the icon. When the operating system finds it, the operating system reads it into working memory (also called loading it) and executes or 'runs' the program. This is why, in the PC world, files that run usually end with ".exe" for execute. Working memory is the place where programs are temporarily stored and where they live as they are running. This is the RAM that you buy when you buy your computer. In it there are millions of places, each with an address, where the program, and we as programmers, can store things.

Pigeonhole Mailbox Named Gus

Imagine that the working memory contains a bunch of pigeonholes, like mailboxes in a post office. To use one of these storage places, here's what we have to do: we need to reserve the spot and name it. Let's pick one and give it a name—how about "Gus?" Then we can use Gus to hold a number, word, or list. Suppose we want to use or change what's in the mailbox. Since we have named the mailbox, we can tell the computer where to find it.

So, how do we go about reserving and naming the storage spot? MicroWorlds has some built-in procedures and operators to assist us. Here they are.

- **Local** reserves and names a storage place;
- **make** puts a value in it; and
- **":"** allows us to grab the value that is in it for us to use.

Let's set up a test program to investigate using **local**, **:**, and **make**.

Test program

Open MicroWorlds, and then open a new project. You can name it **Test.**

Now we will make a little procedure to use to experiment with variables. We'll call our first variable Var1. We want to reserve and name our variable (storage place) using **local,** and then we want to print what's in the storage place using **show.** We also want to put in comments to remind us what we are doing.

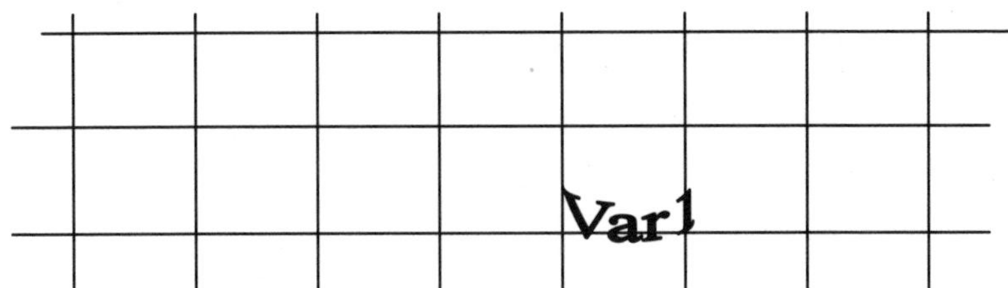

Mailbox Named Var1

Write the following procedure on the procedures page:

```
to TestVar
  local "Var1 ;reserves and names a storage place
  show "Var1  ;we want to print the value in the storage place
end
```

and call it from Main by editing Main to be

```
to Main
  TestVar
end
```

As always, it helps to view the jigsaw puzzles:

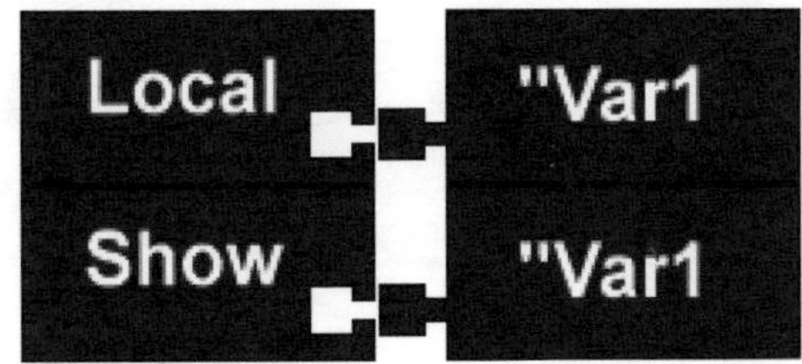

Now go back to your program page 1 and click on the Start button. In the Command Center you will see:

Oops! We didn't expect this. This is the name of the variable (mailbox), not what is in the mailbox (a number).

The built-in procedure **local** is a procedure with one input and no outputs. It tells MicroWorlds to reserve a spot in memory to store things in, and it tells MicroWorlds that we will name this spot **Var1**. It's a little mailbox with an address of **Var1**. So the input to **local** is the name that we want the variable to have.

Show is a very handy procedure that takes one input, a word or a list, and prints it on the Command Center. It is a good procedure to use for experimenting.

I want to know what the value is inside the memory spot named Var1. The line, **show "Var1**, is an instruction to put the word Var1 on the Command Center. This is not really what I meant!

MicroWorlds Logo uses a colon, **:**, as an operator to indicate the *value* stored in the memory spot. So we will say **show :Var1,** meaning *show what's in Var1.*

Change your **TestVar** procedure as follows:

```
to TestVar
   local "Var1  ; reserves and names a storage place
   show  :Var1  ; show what's in Var1
end
```

and run your program. Here is the result I get:

Oops again! We get an error message, telling us that we haven't put a value into the storage space. When we look at our procedure we can see this is true, we made a storage space (a variable) but we didn't tell MicroWorlds what to put it in it. We goofed. **It is a programming error to try to use a value from a variable if none has ever been stored there.**

We have one more procedure to learn and then we can get into some serious variable experimenting. There is a built-in procedure **make** that does the job of storing values in previously named variables. It takes two inputs and has no outputs. The first input is the name of the variable and the second is the value to be stored. It looks like this:

Change your procedure to the following:

```
to TestVar
  local "Var1 ;creates and names a variable
  make "Var1 20 ;puts the value 20 in the variable
  show :Var1 ;prints the value in the variable
end
```

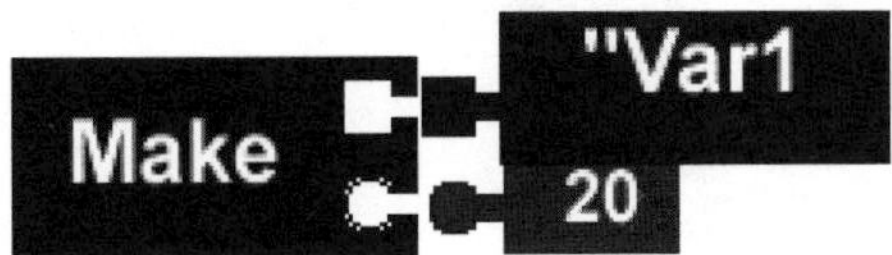

Or, using our mailbox diagram,

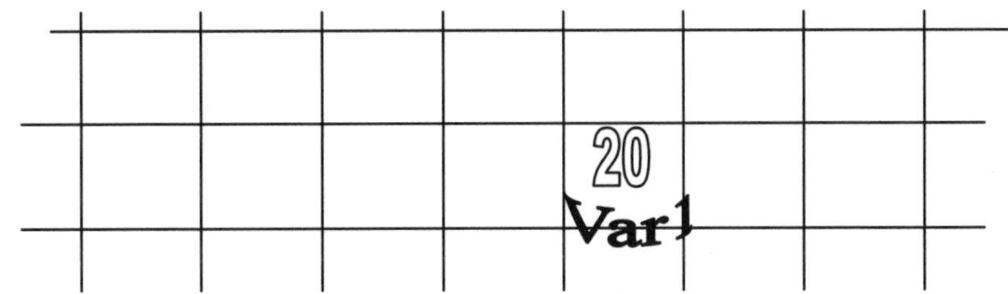

Mailbox With Contents

Lets take a look at what we have in our **TestVar** procedure this time.

We use **local** to make a variable named **Var1**

We use **make** to put the value **20** in the variable.

We use **show** to show **:Var1**, *the value stored in **Var1.***

I think it should all work this time! Before you run your program, so that your Command Center shows only the newest messages, add the **cc** instruction in main, like this:

```
to Main
  cc
  TestVar
end
```

This of course just clears out the Command Center as you start your program each time. Now run your program.

Bingo! The value stored is **20**! Let's also put in **50** and see what happens.

```
to TestVar
  local "Var1
  make "Var1 20
  show :Var1  ; this means show the value stored in Var1
  make "Var1 50
  show :Var1
end
```

Again, using our mailbox diagram,

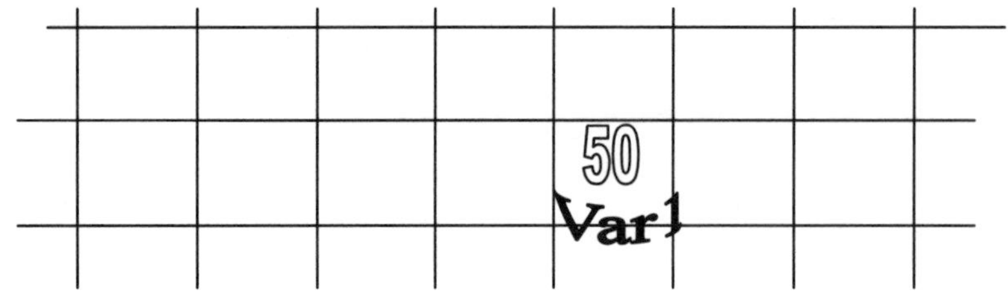

Mailbox With New Contents

We replaced the value stored, and the first one is gone forever.

What about storing a word? Try this:

```
to TestVar
  local "Var1
  make "Var1 20
  show :Var1
  make "Var1 "Me
  show :Var1
end
```

Pretty neat, eh!

Let's make another variable to play with.

```
to TestVar
  local "Var1
  make "Var1 20
  local "Var2
  make "Var2 50
  show :Var1
  show :Var2
end
```

What does your command center look like? It should show 20, then 50. But in this case, there are two mailboxes!

Two Mailboxes With Contents

Here is an arithmetic built-in procedure that is easy to use**, sum**. It takes 2 inputs, both numbers, and has one output (the answer). If you want to add 2 and 3, you would write **sum 2 3**, since outputs come after the procedure name.

Try this:

```
to TestVar
  local "Var1
  make "Var1 20
  local "Var2
  make "Var2 50
  show :Var1
  show :Var2
  show sum 20 15
  show sum :Var1 15
end
```

What's that last line all about? We are adding two numbers. One is the value stored in Var1, and the other is 15. Then we are printing the result. You should get 20 50 35 35.

It is an excellent exercise to draw the jigsaw puzzle form of a line of instruction, especially before you run it. It can really help you learn what's going on. It is neat to see the way the Logo procedures all fit together with their inputs and outputs.

Try adding these lines to **TestVar**. Remember, **sum** has two inputs. Can you tell what they are doing?

```
show sum :Var1 :Var2
show sum :Var1 sum 15 30
```

And of course, make up your own lines to experiment with.

Talk like Logo

Another way to be sure you are understanding how a Logo instruction works is to "talk" your way through an instruction. I will do a couple:

```
show sum 20 15
```

I am MicroWorlds Logo. I see the procedure **show**. This procedure tells me to take one input and put it on the Command Center. I need one input.

- I see the procedure **sum**. It has an output that I can use to satisfy my need for an input. But first I need 2 inputs for **sum** before I can calculate the output.
- I see the procedure **20.** It has one output and no inputs to worry about, great, that is one input to **sum** satisfied.
- I see the procedure **15**. It has one output and no inputs to worry about, great, that is the second input to **sum** satisfied.

- Now I know the output of **sum**, it is **35**
- So now I can satisfy the input to **show**. I will put **35** on the Command Center.

Whew!
One more.

show sum :Var1 sum 15 30

Assume **Var1** holds the value **10**.

I am MicroWorlds Logo. I see the procedure **show.** This procedure tells me to take one input and put it on the Command Center. I need one input.

I see the procedure **sum**. It has an output that I can use to satisfy my need for an input. But first I need 2 inputs for **sum** before I can calculate the output.

I see the phrase **:Var1**. It means *the value stored in* ***Var1***. **:Var1** has an output that I can use to satisfy one of my needs.

I see the procedure **sum.** It has an output that I can use to satisfy my need for an input. But first I need two inputs for **sum** before I can calculate the output.

I see the procedure **15**. It has one output and no inputs to worry about. Great, that is one input satisfied.

I see the procedure **30.** It has one output and no inputs to worry about. Great, that is the second input to **sum** satisfied.

Now I know the output of this last **sum**. It is **45.** So that is my second needed input.

I now have the two inputs to the first sum, namely **10** and **45**, so I can calculate the output of the first sum. It is **55.**

So now I can satisfy the input to **show.** I will put **55** on the Command Center.

I quit!

Exercise:

Write a program that will do the following:

Reserve and name a memory spot called ***size****.*

Store the value of five in the spot.

Reserve and name a memory spot called ***height****.*

Take your height in inches, and store it in the memory spot called ***height****.*

Print the current value of ***size****.*

Print the current value of ***height****.*

Add 3 to the value of ***size*** *and store the result in the same place,* ***size.***

Print the current value of ***size****.*

#17 Logo Animation Using Variables

Type in the following. Save under a new name. It should look like this:

```
====================
to Main

end
====================

to square
   repeat 4 [forward 50 right 90 wait 1]

to Start
   Main
end
```

Now it's time to add an action figure. I want you to add some lines to Main so it looks like this:

```
====================
to Main
   cc
   talkto "t1
   setsh [horse1 horse2 horse3]
   repeat 20 [square]
end
====================
```

Adding an input to our procedure

A while back, I suggested that it would be nice if we could decide how big a square our turtle should make. Then we would have a nice, general procedure that could be used anytime we want a square of any size. You won't believe how easy it is to make this improvement, now that we understand variables.

We want to turn our procedure **square,** which currently has no inputs and no outputs, into a procedure that receives one input. We do that simply by thinking of a good name for the input — how about length?—and putting it on the line that declares the procedure. Since we are passing the *value* in length, we will use **:length**. Make the following change to **square:**

```
to square :length
   repeat 4 [forward 50 right 90 wait 1]
end
```

We just used a shortcut! Instead of using the instruction **local,** we put the variable name in the first line of the procedure. This also takes a spot in memory and names it **length** so we can store a value in it.

Again, using our mailbox diagram,

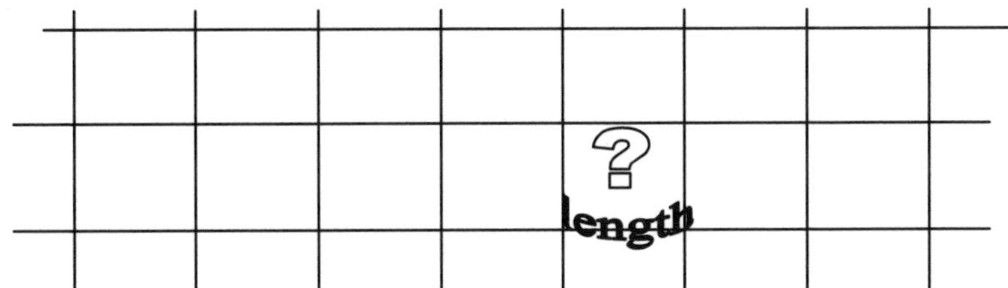

Mailbox With Unknown Contents

The neat thing is that we don't have to use **make** to put the value in. We pass the value to the **square** procedure when we call it. In other words, when we use the **square** procedure, we need to place an input next to it that will go into the mailbox. The code in Main needs to say, for example,

square 30

instead of

square.

The 30 would go into the mailbox named **length**, and wait to be used by the procedure **square**.

So square now needs one input. Its jigsaw piece looks like this now:

Now we need to change **Main** so that when it calls **square,** it satisfies **square's** new need for an input. Let's give it the number **30**. So instead of typing **square,** we will type **square 30**.

```
to Main
   cc
   talkto "t1
   setsh [horse1 horse2 horse3]
   repeat 20 [square 30]
end
```

Now you can try your program and you will find that it works, but it really isn't any better than before. Our revised procedure **square** requires an input, and gets an input, but it doesn't actually use it for anything!

Let's fix **square** so that it makes use of the variable **length.** We want the value stored in **length** to be used as the input to **forward.** Do you remember how? Take a minute to think about it.

To get the value of a variable (the thing in the mailbox), use a colon before the variable name. Change your **square** procedure as follows:

```
to square :length
   repeat 4
     [forward :length right 90 wait 1]
end
```

Now, to find the input for **forward,** Logo must find the value stored in **length.** Where did that value come from? The value is stored there when Main calls the procedure **square** using a number.

Play with your new, more powerful **square** by changing this calling value. Officially this value is called an "*argument.*" (I don't know why. I'm not mad, are you mad?) Inside the procedure the variable is called a *parameter***.**

You can also call **square** directly from the Command Center, for example by typing **square 200** and pressing **Enter.**

We have now finished a very good procedure that we can use any time we want. Here is my finished program**:**

```
============
to Main
   cc
   talkto "t1
   setsh [horse1 horse2 horse3]
   repeat 20 [square 30]
end
==============

to square :length
   repeat 4
     [forward :length right 90 wait 1]
end

to Start
   Main
end
```

Test it! Put in different values for the line in Main that calls square. Use **square 40** and **square 60**. Look over your procedures page and make sure it is free of errors and nice and neat. Then save your project. Now save it again, using File, Save Project As, under the name **Library**. This gives you a handy place to keep all completed procedures. You can copy and paste more procedures into this file in the future, and have them available. If we want to start a new project some time, we just have to copy and paste **Start** and **Main**, and possibly other procedures, from the **Library.**

Our house size can change!

Our next task is to apply what we just learned to the house we made before. We are going to add the capability to re-size the house with a few keystrokes. To draw a house, we go to the Command Center and type **Main**. Now, here's what we want: to get a house twice as big, type in the Command Center **Main 2.** A variable will store the size, 2, and pass it to the procedures as they draw. To get one half as big, type **Main 0.5.** And so on!! If you think about it, you will see that this variable idea is very powerful. In fact, it is a foundational idea for programming. And now you too can do it.

Go to **File Open Project** and load your house file. Rename it, using "save as," calling it "resize house."

The first thing to do is take a procedure, say **triangle**. Let's go through it and re-state all the numbers used for input to **forward** or **back.** You can replace each "forward" or "back" number with a number times one. For example, **forward 50** becomes **forward 50 * 1.** (Put the ones last. This prevents silly errors later.) Note that the computer-ese sign for multiplication is a star, not an x, and that there are spaces between inputs.

Do NOT replace angles, namely the inputs for **right, left**, or **seth**. The angles stay the same even if we make the house twice as big.

Now we are going to replace all those ones with a variable (a spot that holds a value). Let's call the variable **trisize**. To create and name the variable, we will add an argument to the first line of our procedure, like this:

to triangle :trisize

Again, using our mailbox diagram,

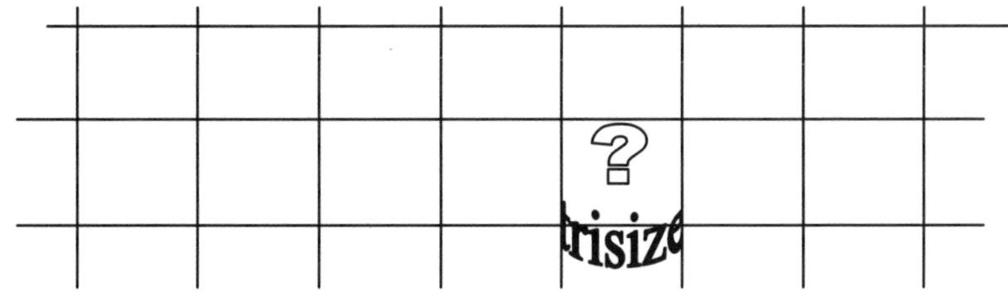

new mailbox for **triangle**

Now we need to change the **triangle** procedure so that we are using the variable **trisize** instead of the number one.

Can you guess how to do that? Let's try this:

```
to triangle :trisize
   ; draws a triangle
   repeat 3 [forward 50 * trisize right 120 wait 1]
end
```

In the command center, type **triangle 5**. You are calling the procedure and passing it a value (an argument). Did that work? Oops, it didn't!

We forgot! In the procedure, we need to tell the computer to get the *value* stored in **trisize!**

Use **:trisize** rather than just **trisize.**

```
to triangle :trisize
   ; draws a triangle
   repeat 3 [forward 50 :trisize right 120 wait 1]
end
```

Now, in the same way, add a variable (you pick the name) to all the procedures except **Main.** First put the variable name, such as doorsize, in the procedure's first line preceded by a colon. Within all procedures, restate **forward** and **back** values as a number * 1, and then replace the 1 with **:doorsize** (or whatever). Don't use the same variable name in two different procedures. This could cause confusion for the computer. We want all our variables to be local—that is, we use the variable name only inside the procedure that creates them.

Test each procedure by typing the procedure name followed by a number into the Command Center.

```
square 2
climb.to.roof 2
triangle 2
door 2
```

See if the computer draws each one properly. Troubleshoot according to your error messages. Sometimes Logo doesn't like the quote marks you use. Make sure they are the double ones. Now instead of 2, use 3 or 4.

Now, let's pull it all together. We want to call the procedures by passing a number from **Main**. Let's set up another variable name to be used within **Main**: how about **housesize**? So, make the first line of **Main** like this:

```
to Main :housesize
```

This creates and names a variable **housesize** to be used in **Main** to pass a value from **Main** to the sub-procedures.

We need to make some more changes in **Main.** Now, in any line where you call a procedure, call it using its name and the value of what is in **housesize:**

(before) **door ; draws a door**

(halfway there) **door 2 ;draws a door twice as big**

(after) **door :housesize ; draws a door the size of the value in housesize**

This puts the value from **housesize** into the mailbox for each procedure's input variable. Let's suppose that the value we are putting in **housesize** is 2. In other words, we type this in the command center:

Main 2

This puts a two in **housesize**, which is the variable we created in **Main.** As the program runs, our code passes the number to the mailboxes (variables) in other procedures, like this:

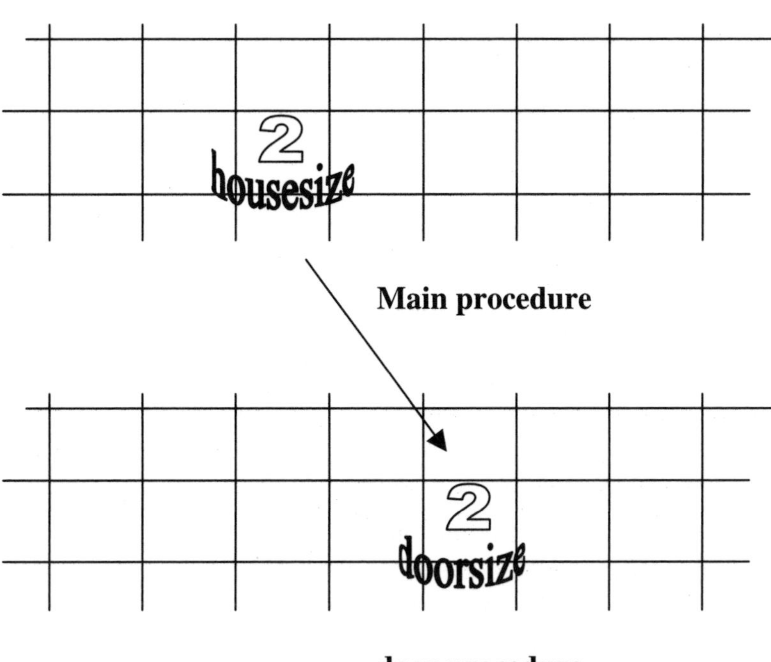

door procedure

Whew! We've made a bunch of changes. To test them, go to the Command Center and type **Main 1.** Does it draw the house as it originally was? Now type **Main 2**. Is it twice as big? for **Main 0.5,** is it half as big?

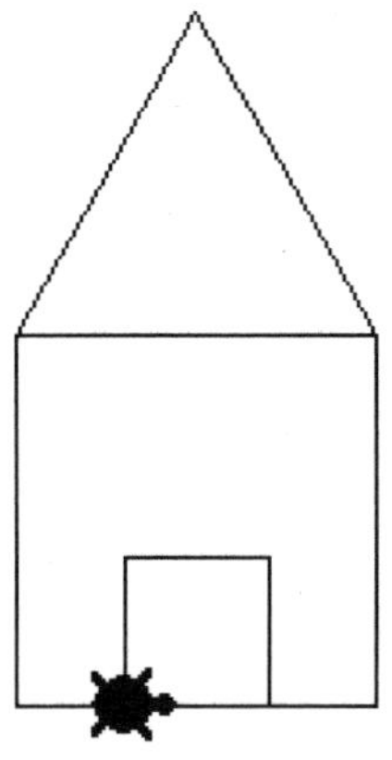

Main 2

Main 0.5

Save it. Show your teacher that it works.

A special project

Since you can do it with the house, you can do it with your building project too, as a special project. This may take a lot of time, depending on how complicated your building is, because you have to make changes to every command that uses **forward** or **back**. Follow the same procedure as for the house. If you are part of a class working on this, someone in the class can volunteer to put the re-sized buildings together, using copy and paste, into one file and draw a cityscape for the class.

#18 Do the Logo Walk

Now, let's do some more animation. I would like to develop a procedure called **walk.**

From the file menu, open your project saved from an earlier lesson called **Square1**. Then from the file menu select "Save Project As" and save your project as **Walkyourname.** On the procedures page, your program should look like this:

```
==================
to Main
  cg
  cc
  talkto "t1
  setsh [horse1 horse2 horse3]
  repeat 20
    [square 30]
end
====================

to square :length
  repeat 4
    [forward :length right 90 wait 1]
end

to Start
  Main
end
```

Our approach

We are going to experiment with making a procedure **walk.** We will start out with a general idea of what we want to do but we will build the procedure bit by bit as we see what works and what doesn't. And we will make mistakes along the way that we will learn from and use to make our procedure better.

After we do **walk,** I would like to do **jump**. Eventually, I would like to make a critter walk along and jump over things.

How do you walk?

In Main, edit the **setsh** line so that it looks like this:

```
setsh [dog1 dog2]
```

I have changed to the two dog shapes, simply because eventually we are going to write a procedure **jump**, and the dogs look better at it! Let's actually sit down and think a bit before we start to write our **walk** procedure. I envision the turtle switching back and forth between two shapes as it moves along. This means that the procedure **forward** must be called more than once. Probably it should be called twice, once for each shape. We learned from **Square** that continuous calls to **forward** without a **wait** don't work very well, so we should include a **wait**.

What about inputs to **walk?** What should we make as a variable? Well, how about making how far to go before changing shapes an input to the procedure?

Okay, enough thinking, let's code!

In the command center, type **cg** to clear the graphics, so we can start fresh. Then type in this procedure in your procedures page.

```
to walk :stepsize
  repeat 2
    [forward :stepsize
    wait 1]
end
```

and edit **Main** to look like this:

```
to Main
  cg
  cc
  talkto "t1
  setsh [dog1 dog2]
  repeat 200
    [walk 5]
end
```

Go to your program page and click on the Start button. How did it go?

My dog went backwards! Yours may be going up or down! We forgot to set the heading of the turtle/dog before we called **walk**. (Remember, the heading is the direction the turtle is facing.) The dog faces the opposite direction from the horse. We forgot one of our programming goals, which I repeat here:

It must work every time for every one. In other words it can't depend on the user doing things in the right order, or depend on the turtle facing the right direction or some other condition. It must account for and handle all those possibilities itself.

How can we do that? We'd like to point the turtle to the left, no matter what it was doing before that. So we need to set the heading, using **seth**, for set heading. Let's try this: Add **seth –90**, or **seth 270** (same thing) to **Main.** This points the turtle to the left, no matter what it was doing before that.

```
to Main
  cg
  cc
  talkto "t1
  setsh [dog1 dog2]
  seth 270
  repeat 200
    [walk 5]
end
```

We want our **walk** to be able to work with any shapes in any direction. That is why we wouldn't add **seth 270** to the **walk** procedure itself. It also makes sense to put it before the **repeat**, because it would be inefficient to call it 200 times. I find the dog a little slow, so let's try increasing the step size to 10. Change **Main** and run your program again.

```
to Main
  cc
  talkto "t1
  setsh [dog1 dog2]
  seth 270
  repeat 200
    [walk 10]
end
```

There, I think that looks pretty good. Now let's do **jump.**

The jump procedure

Well, I guess the obvious variable in a **jump** procedure would be "How high?" or height. So let's get started:

```
to jump :height
  seth 0
  forward :height
  wait 1
  back :height
end
```

What do you think of this procedure? Do you think it will work? Let's add it to **Main** and give it a try. Here is the new **Main:**

```
to Main
   cc
   talkto "t1
   setsh [dog1 dog2]
   seth 270
   repeat 200
      [walk 10
      jump 10]
end
```

Give your program a try.

My dog just kept on going up!

Do you see why? In **jump**, we set the heading of the turtle to up (**seth 0**) but we never set it back again! In other words our **jump** procedure had the unpleasant side effect of changing the direction the turtle was headed. But how do we set it back to its original direction when it is finished jumping? We can't just set the heading to 270, because next time the turtle may be going in some completely different direction and we don't want **jump** to have the side effect of changing the turtle's direction. We want our procedures to do only one thing!

We need another variable, a storage spot to put the heading of the turtle before it jumps. Then, after it jumps, we can pull that value out and point the turtle that way again. Determining the heading is easy, since there is a built-in procedure **heading** which has, as an output, the direction of the turtle. (As a beginner you may be thinking "Yeah, but I didn't know there was a procedure called **heading**, how are you supposed to know these things?" Well, you aren't expected to know, but you need to learn to look. Just go to the Help and browse through the Index looking for words that just might be useful.)

So we can determine the original heading, but how do we store it?

- First, we name a storage location, and
- then we make the value stored there to be the same as the current **heading.**
- Then we do our jump.
- Finally, we read the value stored and
- use it to set the heading again after the jump.

Change your **jump** procedure as follows:

```
to jump :height
   local "originalHeading  ;this is a variable for storing the original heading
   make "originalHeading heading ;this stores the heading in the variable
   seth 0  ;now we prepare to jump up
   forward :height   ; we are jumping
   wait 1
```

```
back :height  ;we are falling back down from the jump
seth :originalHeading  ; we are turning our head to point the way we started
end
```

Do you see how that works? Now try it.

Heh, well it works, but I think there is room for improvement. I would like the dog to walk further before it jumps, so let's change the size of the steps by changing **Main** as follows:

```
repeat 200
  [walk 100
  jump 10]
```

Well, that is interesting but not really what I had in mind. Let's take another look at our **walk** procedure. Here it is again:

```
to walk :stepsize
  repeat 2
    [forward :stepsize
    wait 1]
end
```

What is happening is the Dog is walking along, changing shapes once and then jumping. In order to get it to **walk** more than it jumped we made the stepsize larger (100). But this ruined the animation. What I really want is for the dog to walk along many steps, changing shapes and then to jump. We need to revise our **walk** procedure so that we can control both the step size and the quantity of steps. Let's add another parameter (variable) to our **walk** procedure.

```
to walk :stepsize :qsteps
  repeat :qsteps
    [forward :stepsize
    wait 1]
end
```

Qsteps stands for quantity of steps. Now we can easily control the size of each step and the quantity of steps with each call to **walk**. Change **Main** to make use of this new power and try your program.

```
to Main
  cg
  cc
  talkto "t1
  setsh [dog1 dog2]
  seth 270
  repeat 200
    [walk 10 10
    jump 10]
end
```

There, that's pretty good! I would suggest you play with these procedures for a while and be sure you understand how they work.

The method we just used to develop these procedures should show you that finished projects don't start out as finished projects. You need to try things, adapt them to make them better and sometimes abandon them if you find a better way to accomplish a task.

When you see someone's finished project, don't forget that all projects start out the same way, a blank page. It just takes time and a large amount of perseverance to make them into masterpieces.

Save your work

Be sure to save your work as **Walkyourname**. Here is the complete procedures page:

```
====================
to Main
  cg
  cc
  talkto "t1
  setsh [dog1 dog2]
  seth 270
  repeat 200
    [walk 10 10
    jump 10]
end
====================
to jump :height
  local "originalHeading
  make "originalHeading heading
  seth 0
  forward :height
  wait 1
  back :height
  seth :originalHeading
end

to square :length
  repeat 4
    [forward :length right 90 wait 1]
end

to Start
  Main
end
```

```
to walk :stepsize :qsteps
   repeat :qsteps
      [forward :stepsize
      wait 1]
end
```

Exercises

1. *Make a file called beeyourname.*
2. *Use a bumblebee (bee1, bee2) as your character. Make the bee fly across the screen and wobble downward and back up, and repeat the whole thing a number of times.*
3. *Be able to change the number of steps or wing movements between down-wobbles. Show a teacher the results of changing this.*
4. *For grins: replace the bee with a snake (snake1, snake2).*
5. *Make the bee or snake go forward, then wobble up and back, then go forward, then wobble down and back. Repeat the whole thing a number of times.*
6. *Extra credit: Make the bee fly like this repeatedly:*

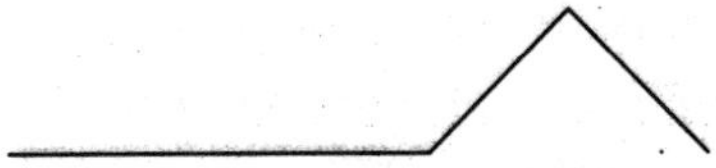

Save your work in at least two places.

#19 Debugging Jump

Eventually I want a **jump** routine that we can use to make a character appear to jump over obstacles. Right now we have the character jumping at regular intervals. For our next improvement, let's add a **jump** button so the character will jump when we click the button.

Load in your work

From the file menu, open your project named **Walkyourname**. Then from the file menu select "Save Project As" and save your project as **Jumpyourname**

In the procedures page, your program should look like this:

```
====================
to Main
  cg
  cc
  talkto "t1
  setsh [dog1 dog2]
  seth 270
  repeat 200
    [walk 10 10
    jump 10]
end
========================
to jump :height
  local "originalHeading
  make "originalHeading heading
  seth 0
  forward :height
  wait 1
  back :height
  seth :originalHeading
end

to square :length
  repeat 4
    [forward :length right 90 wait 1]
end

to Start
  Main
end
```

```
to walk :stepsize :qsteps
  repeat :qsteps
    [forward :stepsize
    wait 1]
end
```

Add a button

We now have three movement procedures, but we are not really using the **square** procedure at this point. Our **jump** procedure seems to work very well when we call it from **Main**. Now I want the character to jump when I push a button! And only when I push a button!

First, ***let's add a button.*** In the icon bar, click on the finger pushing the button and then drag on the page to make the button.

A dialog box pops up giving us the opportunity to type in the instruction that we want to run when the button is clicked. Also, the name of the instruction becomes the label on the button. I want the label to be **jump**, so type in **jump** as the name of the instruction.

If you need to resize the button, drag an area on the program page that includes all of the button, then release the mouse button. The button should then have four handles (little boxes) on it which allow you to resize it. Put the mouse arrow on it, and push and hold the mouse button down while moving the handle to a different place. This changes the size of the picture. You can also delete the button when the handles are showing by pushing the delete button on the keyboard.

Drag the **jump** button down beside the start button. Try clicking on the **jump** button. What response do you get? The program tries to run our **jump** procedure directly, bypassing Main.

Hmm, we get an error message. Our **jump** procedure requires an input. But where do we put the input? I really don't want to have to go to the dialog box of the **jump** button to change the arguments for **jump** every time I want to try something different. Here's a solution—let's change the name of the **jump** procedure to something slightly different. Also, we want to change **Main** so that it no longer calls **jump**. Let's change the name of our **jump** procedure to **doJump** and remove the call to **jump** from **Main**. Make your procedures page look like this:

```
====================
  to Main
    cc
    talkto "t1
    setsh [dog1 dog2]
    seth 270
    repeat 200
        [walk 10 10] ;get rid of the call to jump
  end
=====================
```

```
to doJump :height ; change the name from jump to doJump
   local "originalHeading
   make "originalHeading heading
   seth 0
   forward :height
   wait 1
   back :height
   seth :originalHeading
end


to Start
   Main
end

to walk :stepsize :qsteps
   repeat :qsteps
      [forward :stepsize
      wait 1]
end
```

Try your program by clicking on the Start button. The dog walks (actually runs but we'll call it walk) across the screen. Click on the **jump** button. You get an "I don't know how to Jump" error message, because there is no longer a **jump** procedure. We renamed it to **doJump.**

Processes

There is one other thing to notice. Even though you get an error message, the little dog keeps on walking! We get the error message because when we click on the button, we call the procedure **jump** which does not exist any more. Doesn't that strike you as a bit strange that the dog keeps walking? We have an error, but the program keeps running! Let's try a little experiment. I'll call this Version 1 of the program.

Let's put the same error in **Main,** calling **jump,** and see what happens. Stop your dog and then edit **Main**, putting a call to **jump** back in, as follows:

```
repeat 200
     [Walk 10 10
   Jump 30]
```

We will call that Version 2 of the program. Now, after the dog **walks** 10 steps, the program will call **jump**, which does not exist. On your program page, Click on **Start**. Sure enough, you get the error message but this time the dog stops.

What is going on here?

The explanation is that the Logo language has "processes." Each process is independent of another process. A process is almost like its own little program. When we click on a button we start a process. If we had more than one turtle moving along on the screen, each one would be running in its own process. In Version 1 of the program, clicking on the **Start** button started a process which had no errors and ran fine. Clicking on the **jump** button started another process which did have an error and would not run but did not affect the first process.

In Version 2, we put an error in the process that is started by the **Start** button and sure enough, the error stopped the process!

This was just to give you a brief idea about processes. Let's go back to Version 1. Take the call to **jump** out of **Main**.

Jump has a bug!

We need a new procedure **jump** which will be called when the button is clicked. Add this procedure to your Procedures Page:

```
to jump
  doJump 20
end
```

This gives us a way to pass a number to **doJump**. Now try your program. Well, it is fun. You can make the dog **walk** along and then, by clicking on **jump**, make him take a little jump and then carry on. This way we get to have the label we want on the button and we get to keep the program out where we can see it on the Procedures Page.

Did you notice something odd? Did you notice that the dog kept getting higher and higher after we click **jump**? It didn't seem to come all the way back down after a **jump**.

Well, folks, we have a bug in our program. Something is not right, and we need to debug our program. That is, we need to find what the error is. To debug a program, the first step is to find out exactly what is causing the problem.

Let's try to narrow it down. When the turtle just **walks**, it does not move higher.

Try stopping the **walk** (by clicking again on the Start button) and just clicking on the **jump** button. **Jump** seems to work just fine and **walk** seems to work just fine when they are run separately. But when both processes are running at the same time, we seem to have a bug in our program!

So, it only occurs when both processes are running at the same time. I would like to see the movement without the shape of the dog obscuring the turtle. In **Main,** put a semicolon in front of the setsh line, like this:

```
;  setsh [dog1 dog2]
```

The computer sees a line with a semicolon on it and considers it a comment, not part of the program. It is like all the words to the right of the semi-colon are invisible to Logo and just visible to humans. So we have just made this line invisible to Logo. (We "commented the line out.")

Let's turn the dog back into a turtle. ***In MicroWorlds 2.0,*** go to the shape center and click on the little black turtle. Then click on the dog on the program page. ***In MicroWorlds EX***, type a command in the command center: **setsh 0 <enter>.**

Now run the program. Seeing it this way, with the naked turtle, makes me a little suspicious of what is happening with **forward.** Sometimes the turtle points up, sometimes left.

Let's take a hard look at our two procedures and try to figure out what happens that is different, when both procedures are running at the same time.

You can see that both **walk** and **doJump** tell the turtle to move **forward. Forward** just means "go in the direction your head is pointing." So, if the **doJump** process is running, then the head is pointed up (**seth 0**). So during the time the **doJump** process is running, the **walk** process actually calls **forward** and increases the height of the jump! That is why the turtle edges a little higher each time, I THINK! We need to test this theory.

Looking at **doJump,** we see that the turtle's head is pointing up right from the line **seth 0** until the line **seth :originalHeading .** If the turtle spent less time pointing up, would the amount the turtle kept climbing decrease? In other words, let's say the turtle spends time with its head pointing up, and the climbing problem decreases. Then that would confirm our suspicion that the problem is **walk** calling **forward,** while **doJump** has the turtle's head pointing up. It's like the turtle has two bosses who are issuing different orders, and the turtle tries to obey them both.

Let's also decrease the amount of time by getting rid of the **wait 1** line. "Comment out" that line too, as shown below.

```
to doJump height
  local "originalHeading
  make "originalHeading heading
  seth 0
  forward :height
;  wait 1
  back :height
  seth :originalHeading
end
```

Get the turtle walking and then click **jump** several times. On my system, that eliminates the "climbing up" problem! Unfortunately you can barely see the turtle **jump,** but we know that it is. Another way to test is to change **wait 1** to **wait 3** and see if it makes the problem worse. Try it.

Now we understand that the problem is that while the turtle is pointing up in **doJump, walk** makes it go higher. But how are we going to fix it?

Let's eliminate the use of **forward** in the procedure **doJump.** This might solve the problem. It would be nice if we could make the turtle jump without turning its head at all. Then **walk** could make it go forward at the same time without any bad effect. As computer programmers, our next step is to check the Logo Vocabulary in the Help menu to see if there are any other built-in procedures that we could try.

Using ycor

Way down at the bottom of the Index are **xcor** and **ycor**. **Ycor** looks like a very likely candidate, so read the help screen, which is reproduced below:

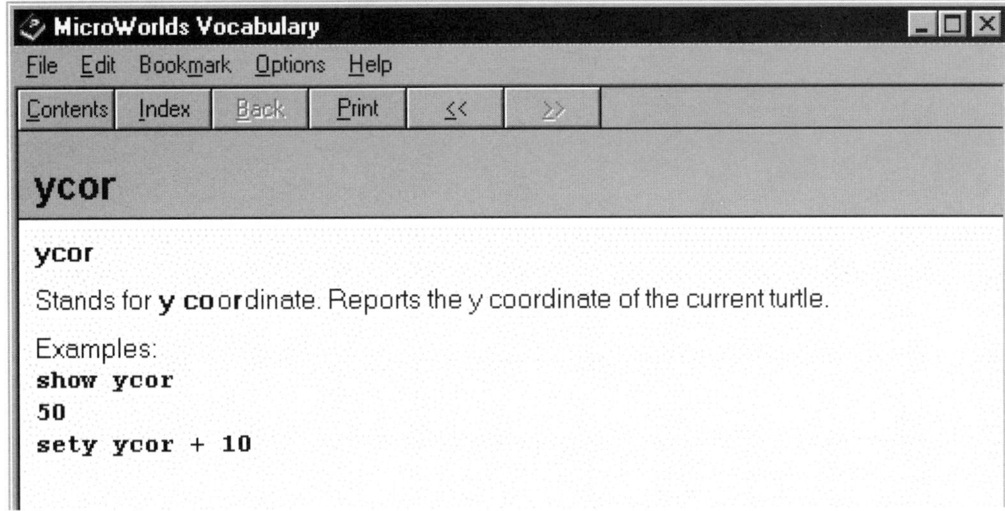

MicroWorlds Vocabulary

File Edit Bookmark Options Help

Contents | Index | Back | Print | << | >>

ycor

ycor

Stands for **y coor**dinate. Reports the y coordinate of the current turtle.

Examples:

```
show ycor
50
sety ycor + 10
```

This tells us that there is a built-in procedure **ycor** that has as an output the y coordinate (height on the screen) of the turtle. There is another procedure **sety** which takes a number as an input and presumably sets the y coordinate.

How might this help us?

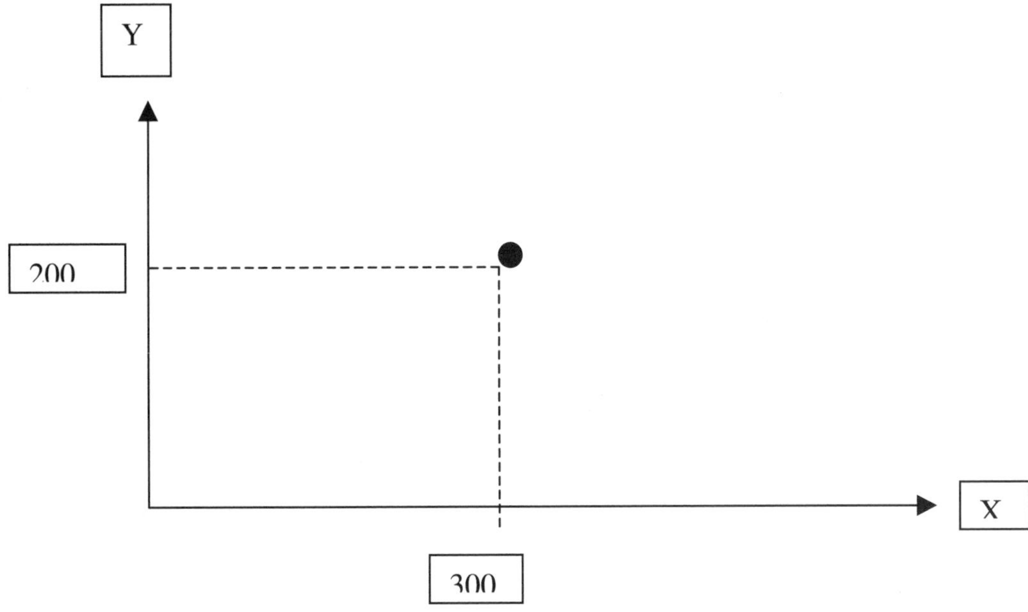

In this little picture, our dot has an address. Its "x coordinate" (sideways position on the screen) is 300. Its "y coordinate" (height on the screen) is 200. These numbers tell us just where we are on the screen, like a street address. It's just like Star Trek or Star Wars, reporting your position using coordinates!

Let's say x=200, y=300 is the address for our turtle. What if we move the turtle up on the screen a little way?

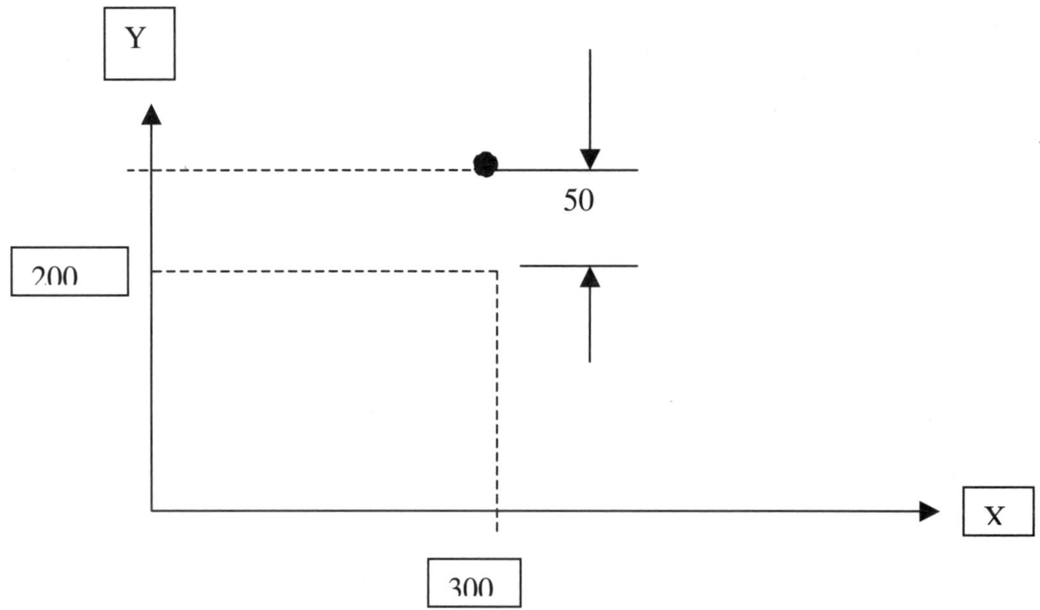

We moved the turtle upward by 50 units. So its y coordinate has changed from 200 to 250. Its x coordinate is still the same.

Suppose we want to move it back to the same spot as before. We would know exactly where to tell it to go if we made a pigeonhole mailbox to save the first y coordinate and could pull that information out when we needed it. Let's:

- **make a pigeonhole and save the y coordinate of the first position**
- **move the turtle to a spot where we have added 50 to the y coordinate**
- **wait a little**
- **pull out the y coordinate of the first position**
- **and move the turtle back to that.**

Let's cast that into Logo. Can you do it on your own and then check your answer with mine? Turn the page when you are ready.

Here's mine:

```
local "originalY
make "originalY ycor
sety sum ycor 50
wait 1
sety :originalY
```

We can now make a few more adjustments. Let's make it really make it interesting by changing the jump of 50 units to a variable, **height,** that is passed to our procedure. So we add code to:

- **create a pigeonhole to store the value for** height **of jump**
- **create a pigeonhole and save the y coordinate of the first position**
- **move the turtle to a location where we have added the value in** height **to the y coordinate**
- **pulled out the y coordinate of the first position from its pigeonhole**
- **and move the turtle back to that.**

Again, write down what you think before you look at what I came up with on the next page!

It is quite common to want to re-write a procedure on a trial basis, but you don't want to lose the old one, at least not yet. Here is what I do. I rename the existing procedure to, say, **doJumpOld** and write the new procedure as **doJump**. That way you do not have to search through your program to change all the calls to **doJump**. They stay as they are, only now they are calling your new version of **doJump**. Then, when we're sure we've made a good change, we can get rid of **doJumpOld.**

Here are my old and my new **doJump**. You really should try to write your own before looking at mine.

```
to doJumpOld :height
  local "originalHeading
  make "originalHeading heading
  seth 0
  forward :height
 ; wait 1
  back :height
  seth :originalHeading
end
```

Work on yours before you turn the page!

```
to doJump :height
   local "originalY
   make "originalY ycor
   sety sum ycor :height
   wait 1
   sety :originalY
end
```

Does it work? How do you change the height of the jump?

Remember to change the number used when calling **doJump** from **Jump**.

I like it! I like our new version of **doJump,** and it has fixed the "climbing up" problem. Time to tidy up our program and save it. Here is my version**:**

```
====================
to Main
   cc
   talkto "t1
   setsh [dog1 dog2]
   seth 270
      repeat 200
         [Walk 10 10]
      end
======================
to doJump :height
   local "originalY
   make "originalY ycor
   sety sum ycor :height
   wait 1
   sety :originalY
end

 to jump
   doJump 40
end

to Start
   Main
end

to walk :stepsize :qsteps
   repeat :qsteps
      [forward :stepsize
      wait 1]
end
```

Exercises

1. *Create a file called hop**yourname,** based on the work you did for this lesson. In it, add to your **jump** program a procedure called "**hop**" that*
   - *Makes the dog hop sideways and back when you push a button called "**hop**."*
   - *Does not use "**forward**."*
   - *Uses variables. Show your dog with two different sizes of hops.*
2. *Change your dog to a horse. Change the code so that the animal is facing right and walks forward when you push start.*
3. *Change the size of the animal's steps and the number of steps it takes when you push start.*
4. *Change the walk procedure so that it doesn't use forward either.*

#20 Cool Animation

Load in your work

From the file menu, open your project named **jumpyourname**. Then from the file menu select "Save Project As" and save your project as **jump2yourname.**

In the procedures page, your program should look like this:

```
==========================
to Main
   cc
   talkto "t1
   setsh [dog1 dog2]
   seth 270
   repeat 200
        [Walk 10 10]
end
==========================
to doJump :height
   local "originalY
   make "originalY ycor
   sety sum ycor :height
   wait 1
   sety :originalY
end

to jump
   doJump 30
end

to Start
   Main
end

to walk :stepsize :qsteps
   repeat :qsteps
      [forward :stepsize
      wait 1]
end
```

Become a master of illusions

Programming often involves creating an illusion. Often you will want to make a creature appear to walk or jump. Actually all you do is move the turtle, change the shape, move the turtle, change the shape. But to the user it creates the illusion that the creature is walking.

If you are using Windows, take a close look at your screen, especially the edges of the windows. It really looks 3-dimensional, doesn't it? It looks like the edge has some depth to it. But it is just an illusion. The screen is flat and two- dimensional. It is just the careful use of light and dark colors to create the illusion of shadowing that makes the screen look three-dimensional.

I want to make a program that makes it look like a creature is jumping over an obstacle. To do this we need to trigger the **doJump** procedure. I am going to program a color to call **doJump** and then plant that color in front of the obstacle. This will create the illusion that when the creature gets near the obstacle, it sees it and jumps over it!

Program a color

MicroWorlds has a really cool and useful feature that allows you to program colors. You can program a procedure to be called if a turtle touches that color, or a different procedure if the mouse clicks on that color. We will be using the turtle rule here.

In Microworlds 2.0, go to your program page and switch to the drawing center. Click on the gray color. You will see this dialog box:

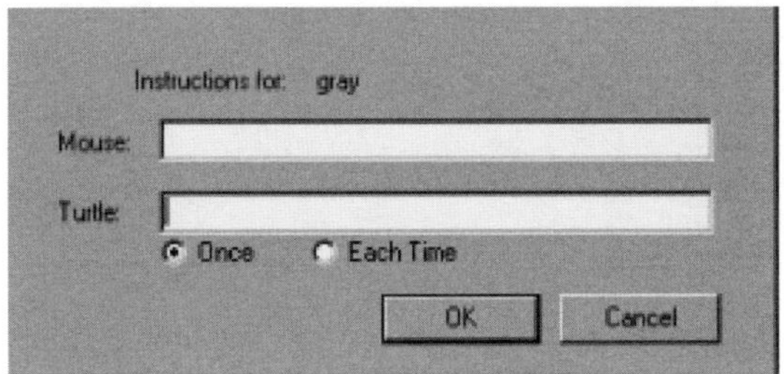

In Microworlds EX, click on the paintbrush icon to see the **painting/clipart window.** Make sure the paintbrush icon at the top of the window is pushed. Right-click on a color in the spectrum, for example gray. A little button comes up that says "edit gray." Click on that button, and the color dialog box shown above appears.

Here you see that you can put an instruction inside this dialog box that the computer will run when a turtle touches the gray color. It goes next to the word "turtle" in the dialog box. Leave the line next to "mouse" empty.

The color gray is an **object,** as is a turtle. An object has properties. In the real world, objects have properties. For example, if I jump on a trampoline, I bounce back. This is a property of a trampoline, not a sidewalk. In cyberworld, colors can have properties. If a turtle hits a color, it activates a procedure that you choose: bouncing back is certainly a possibility. We haven't written the procedure yet, but we will fill in the property in the dialog box anyway. In the white area next to Turtle: type **colorGrayHit** and click on OK. We will write this procedure in a second.

While you are in the Drawing Center and the gray color is selected, click on the spray can and spray a good solid gray splotch of color on the program page. Then go back to the Command Center.

ColorGrayHit

Go to the Procedures page, and we will program the color gray to call **doJump**. Write the procedure **colorGrayHit** as follows:

```
to colorGrayHit
  doJump 50
end
```

Now go back to the program page and click on the **Start** button. Make sure your dog hits the gray splotch. Isn't that neat? My little dog jumps up and down a few times in the gray and then continues on its way. If yours isn't doing it, add more gray. You can do this by spraying more gray, or drawing a fat gray line, in the dog's path of course.

Jump a pond

Let's put a pond for the dog to jump over. You do this by hatching another turtle and placing him where you want the pond. Then you go to the Shape Center and click on the Pond, then the Turtle. Here is the center of my screen.

Try the program. For me, the results are pretty good, but we have two problems to fix. One is that it would be much better if the dog jumped forward, and with one jump cleared the pond. The other problem, which wouldn't be as noticeable if we fixed problem one, is that the dog disappears behind the pond. It would look better if the dog were in front of the pond. Let's fix the second problem first. Oh, and one more thing. You could delete the Jump button, since it was only a temporary thing, used to help us test our procedure.

Who's on first?

In MicroWorlds, the most recently hatched turtle goes in front of any other turtles. Also the turtles are automatically named **t1**, **t2** and so on. In our case, this is not the order we want. The only way I know of changing this is to just accept it and change turtles. In other words, we will make our dog **t2** and our pond **t1**. To see what a particular turtle's name is, right-click on the turtle.

On the program page, drag the **t2**/pond out of the way and drag the **t1**/dog into the middle of the gray splotch. Then go to the shapes center and be sure the pond is still selected. Click on the **t1**/dog. This should now make the first turtle, **t1**, look like the pond. Now go to the procedures page. We need to change our **talkto** line so that we are now talking to **t2**. Change **Main** as shown:

```
to Main
  cc
  talkto "t2
  setsh [dog1 dog2]
  seth 270
  repeat 200
    [Walk 10 10]
end
```

Give the program a try. There, that solves problem two. What do you think would be the way to solve problem one?

Go the distance

I think we need to either change our procedure **doJump** or to make a different procedure that both jumps up and forward. I like the first option of revising our existing procedure **doJump** and making it more flexible. We will try to make it so that it can be used both to jump up and down and to jump over something.

To jump over an object, the turtle needs to move up and also move forward a certain amount. We need a second input to **doJump** so we can control how far forward the turtle should move while it is jumping. Let's think like this:

> We will need two variables or mailboxes to store two values, height and a new one—how about distance?
>
> We'll set up a local variable, originalY, to hold the original y coordinate value.
>
> We'll put the original y coordinate in there.
>
> Now we'll set the y coordinate to a new number, the sum of the old one and the value in height. We'll wait a second.
>
> Now we need to move forward to clear the pond. How about going forward by the amount stored in the variable/mailbox distance? Then wait a sec.
>
> Then set the y coordinate back to the original value.

Can you set up some Logo code to match this line of reasoning? Try it. Then turn the page to look at mine, and see if yours is different.

Here is my **doJump**:

```
to doJump :height :distance
   local "originalY
   make "originalY ycor
   sety sum ycor :height
   wait 1
   forward :distance
   wait 1
   sety :originalY
end
```

We also need to change where we call **doJump**, to reflect two variables instead of one.

```
to colorGrayHit
   doJump 50 100
end
```

It works! Finally we have a great little procedure that can be used to make turtles jump over things.

You will notice that your jump button doesn't work right any more. To fix that, have it call doJump using two variables instead of one. How about this?

```
to jump
   doJump 30 30
end
```

You should copy your **doJump** procedure into your Library file.

Launching skaters

Before I end this lesson, let's have a little fun. Hatch another turtle and put it in line with your gray splotch. This turtle is automatically named **"t3."** You can check this by right-clicking on it.

I would like to use the skater shapes-- **skater1, skater2 and skater3--**at the same time as the dog. How about if we modify the end of **Main** to add a section that says talk to **t3**, set shape to skater1, skater2, and skater3, and use the **walk** procedure to make it skate?

You definitely should try to program this on your own before looking at mine, but don't spend too much time on it because there is a bit of information that we have not talked about yet.

(Which way did your skater go the first time you tried your solution? Mine too! :-)

Here is my 'first try' which does not work right:

```
===========================
to Main
  cc
  talkto "t2
  setsh [dog1 dog2]
  seth 270
  repeat 200
    [walk 10 10]
  talkto "t3
  setsh [skater1 skater2 skater3]
  seth 90
  repeat 200
    [walk 10 10]
end
===========================
```

When you try this program, you will see that the dog continues to do its thing properly, but the other turtle never moves. Perhaps the dog is walking too many times. Change your **Main** as follows:

```
===========================
to Main
  cc
  talkto "t2
  setsh [dog1 dog2]
  seth 270
  repeat 5
    [walk 10 10]
  talkto "t3
  setsh [skater1 skater2 skater3]
  seth 90
  repeat 200
    [walk 10 10]
end
===========================
```

Try it and let it run for a few minutes. First the dog correctly does its thing and then the skater does her thing. If you follow the lines in Main, this makes sense. The repeat procedure causes the program to run the following list of instructions [Walk 10 10] over and over and then proceeds to the next line.

But what we really want is for a process to be launched making the dog walk and then for the program to continue to the next line and launch another process to make the skater walk, **at the same time**. This can be done using the built-in procedure **launch. Launch** has as an input a list of instructions to run as a separate process. Change your **Main** as follows:

```
========================
to Main
   cc
   talkto "t2
   setsh [dog1 dog2]
   seth 270
   launch
      [
      repeat 200
         [walk 10 10]
      ]
   talkto "t3
   setsh [skater1 skater2 skater3]
   seth 90
   launch
      [
      repeat 200
         [walk 10 10]
      ]
end
=========================
```

There! Pretty cool, eh! Be sure to save your work. This program launches two processes that operate independently.

Who are you talking to?

One more thing to notice about this program is that **colorGrayHit** automatically seems to run the line **talkto "whatEverTurtleTouchedMe** before it calls the procedure **doJump.** This functionality is built-in to the MicroWorlds Logo language.

Exercise your skills

Learning how to program is a bit like learning how to ride a bike. Your teacher can tell you how to do it; others can show you how to do it; and you can read about it. But there is only one way to learn how and that is to do it. You have learned quite a few built-in procedures now and some programming techniques. Now you should consolidate your knowledge by actually putting these things to use.

I suggest you take the time to write several of your own procedures now. Even rewrite the same ones we have done. Do them over and over until you can do them totally without looking at the code here.

Make up your own little projects but don't let them get too complex. If you are banging in to a wall, ditch the project and do a different one. There are still lots of things you don't know about Logo and, in time, that wall will be dissolved.

Exercises

1. *Save your file under jump2yourname. Now save it again as tornadoyourname.*
2. *Modify the file so as to make the following things happen at the same time as the dog running and jumping and the skater skating:*
    - *Place another turtle, t4 , in the shape of a castle in the lower right corner of the picture.*
    - *Yet another turtle, t5, takes the shapes of tornado1 and tornado2 and moves to the right toward the castle.*
    - *Spray-paint some blue near the castle. When it strikes the blue, the tornado jumps over the castle.*
    - *When the tornado jumps, the castle turns into a cloud and then back into a castle.*
    - *Extra credit: turn the castle randomly into other shapes when the tornado strikes.*
3. *In a new file, draw a maze with the drawing palette, using blue lines. Using the same idea as colorGrayHit, set up a turtle proceeding through your maze. Start it with a start button.*

#21 Supercharge Your Browser

What is a plug-in?

A very smart programming trick is to make a program that can be altered, or upgraded, after it has been delivered to the user. That is what Microsoft and Netscape have done with their browsers.

If a company wants Web surfers to be able to see their program's files in the surfer's web browsers, then the company can write a plug-in to be added to the browser. The plug-in adds a further capability to the browser. Web browsers (Microsoft Internet Explorer and Netscape) have the built-in functionality to display different types of files such as html, jpg, gif and java applets. With plug-ins, you can extend the capabilities of your browser to view other file types. One popular example of a plug-in is Shockwave.

The programmers for MicroWorlds have built a plug-in. If you download and install the plug-in (instructions to follow) then you can actually run a MicroWorlds project right in your browser, animation and everything! It is very cool.

Getting the plug-in

As soon as you say "download", a lot of people say to themselves "Oh, that's too technical for me!" and leave. Did you realize that you successfully downloaded any text that you have read on the Internet? That's right, a page is 'downloaded' from a Web server to your computer and, because it is an HTML file, your browser knows how to display it. Downloading just means moving from a Web server to your computer.

When you download an HTML file or a jpg or a gif, they are displayed in your browser. If you try to download an exe (executable) file, Netscape or Internet Explorer assume you want to save it to disk and will ask you where you want to save it.

I am going to walk you step by step through the process of getting and installing the plug-in. The actual link to get it is after the instructions.

Here are the instructions:

First, go to www.microworlds.com. Select the icon at the lower left for downloading the MicroWorlds 2.0 plug-in.

When you click on a link to get (download) a program, Netscape (or Internet Explorer) realizes that it cannot display the information in your browser window. What it does next depends on how your browser is set. You may see this box or you may jump right to the next.

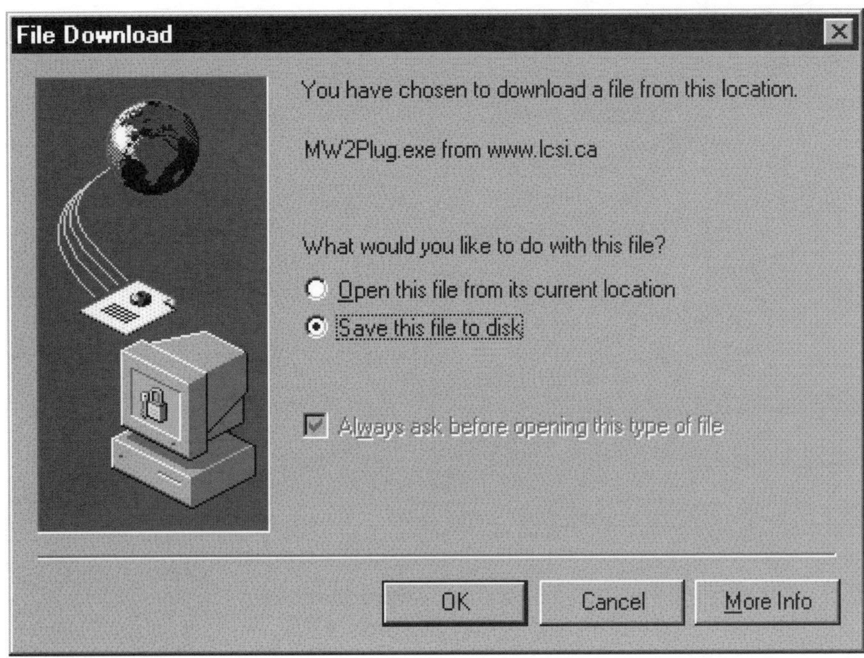

If you see this box, select "Save this file to disk" and click on OK.

Now your browser needs to be told where to save it. So, when you click on the link at the bottom of the page, your browser will show you the 'Save as..." box.

The box will look something like this.

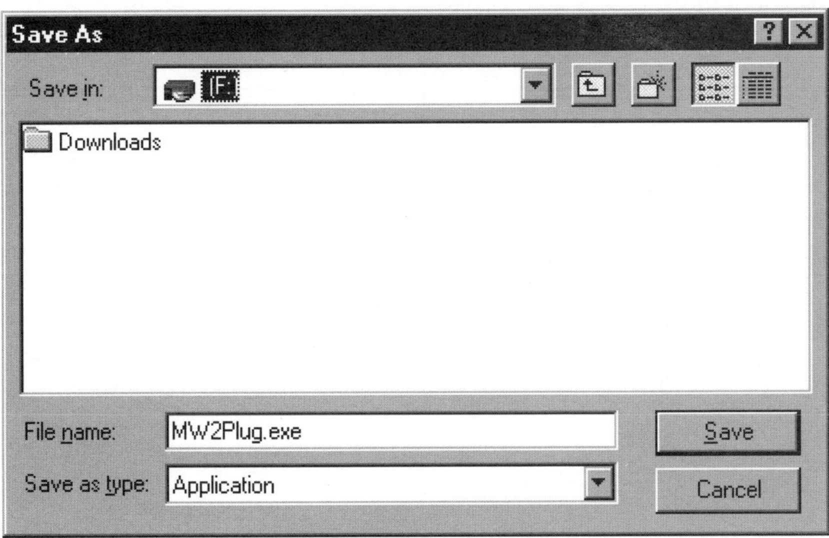

This is a standard Windows "Save As" box.

You need to select a location to save the file you are about to get - and there is one very easy place to save it, which I will show you in a minute.

Click on the little down arrow as shown below.

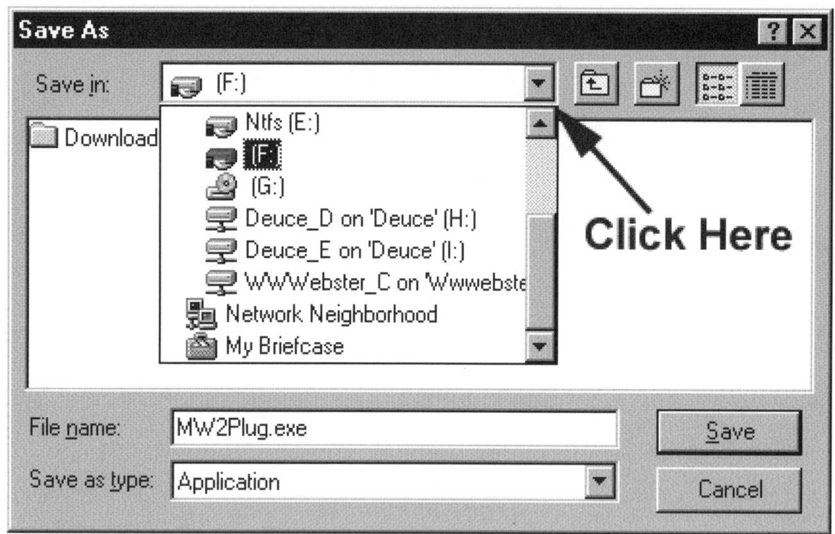

Yours of course will look quite different than mine, but you can get the idea.

Now click on the top of the scrollbar, if you have a scrollbar, until "Desktop" is visible at the top, as shown here.

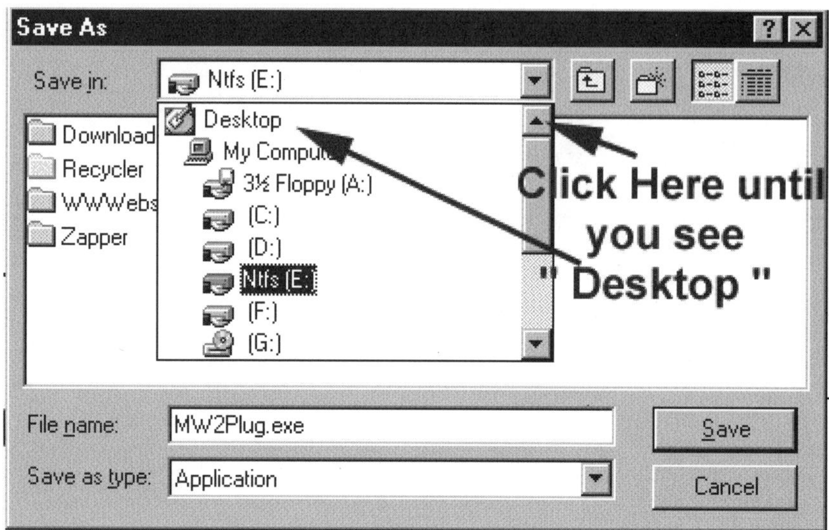

and then click on Desktop to select it.

and finally the little "Save As..." box should look like this:

Notice, in the box named **File name** is the name of the file you are going to download, namely **MW2Plug.exe** and you are going to save it right on your desktop! This will put an icon where you can see it on the desktop.

Click on the Save button and you will see a window like this:

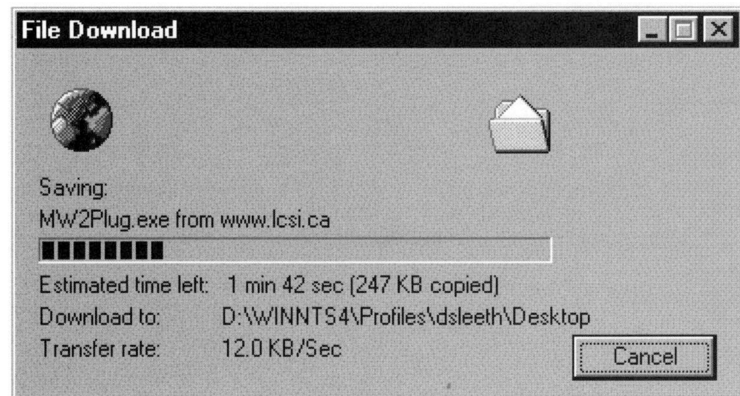

When the "Saving" box disappears and you see

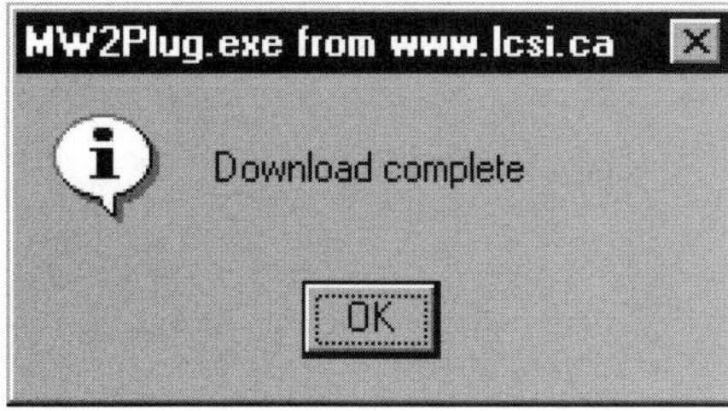

Click on OK. Then close Netscape and logoff the Internet. Close all programs, one by one, until you can see your desktop. On your desktop somewhere will be the MW2Plug.exe icon. Here is a picture of how mine looked.

Now you have downloaded the plug-in, saved it on your hard drive and are ready to install it. Be sure to close all programs.

Then double click on the MW2Plug.exe icon.

This starts the standard installation program. Just follow the instructions (for me, it just means clicking on 'Next' twice and then OK).

After the plug-in is installed, you can log back on to the Internet and test your newly super-charged browser!

Now Test It

Go to www.microworlds.com to the MicroWorlds Project Library. This time, download any of the projects that others have put there. Play with them and guess how they work. Pick one to work on yourself.

Appendix I: Web Site Construction Plans

Skyscraper Web site

Here is a detailed plan for the skyscraper Web site for our co-op, which has two computer science classes (jr. high school and high school). We entered the St. Louis Junior Academy of Science Cyberchallenge competition, novice division. You may be able to check out our Cyberchallenge entries on the Web site at http://www.jracademy.com/~wheeleh/ and http://www.jracademy.com/~harrism/.

How Do You Design a Skyscraper?

Creative Home Educators' Co-op, Sr. High

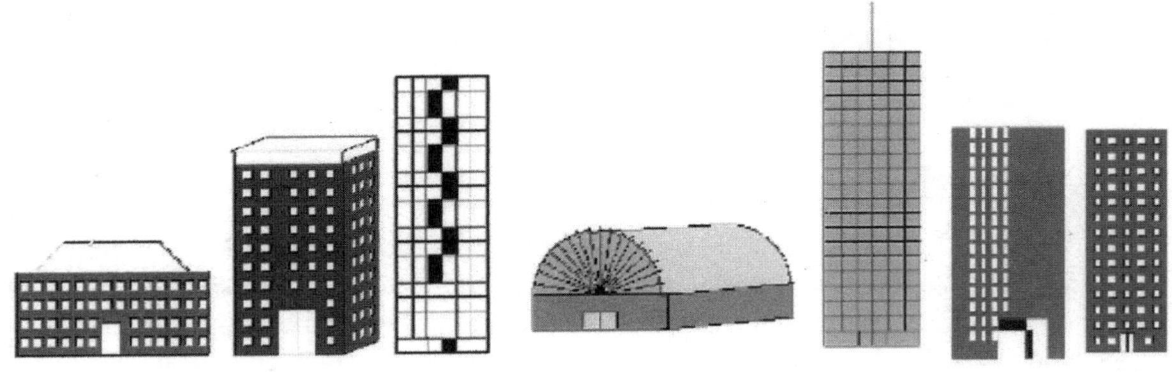

History
Wind
Stone
Windows
Flexibility
A Historic Skyscraper
Do This Experiment!
Just for fun!

Research assignments for Skyscraper Web sites

We will be creating two Web sites, one for each class. For the Cyberchallenge competition, we will inform our viewers about a topic in applied science that we have researched and illustrated. Since we have already created skyscraper illustrations that we can use on our Web sites, let's learn more about skyscrapers!

Each homeschooler will create a Web page on a topic concerning skyscraper design, including a picture. We will have a home (index) page for each class that calls the pages of the people in the class.

Here are Cyberchallenge requirements:

- All material should be your own creation, or you must have permission to use it. Use proper spelling and grammar.
- We are teaching information related to applied science (skyscrapers).
- The site should demonstrate an activity that visitors may use and learn from.
- The site must have links to other sites that are good resources. When a visitor takes one of these links, we must provide a pop-up message that informs visitors that by following the link they will be leaving the Academy of Science server.
- The site needs to direct visitors to send questions via email to someone@somewhere.com

Week 1 Assignments

Each student needs to answer one of the questions below, researching the topic and writing it up on a word processor. Be sure you save the file for later. Look up at least three different sources on your question. Jr. high --Write 10 to 15 sentences about it. Sr. high--write 25 sentences about it. Do a good job of writing! For both classes, include the sources in a bibliography at the end. If the source is a Web site, include the URL and also any information you can figure out about who posted the Web site and who wrote the article. If you know an engineer or architect, you can ask that person and write down the answers. Here is a good place to start: www.pbs.org/wgbh/buildingbig

Individual students, take your topic from the following lists.

Jr. High Site: What is a skyscraper made of?

- What keeps a skyscraper from flopping over?
- Why does a skyscraper need to be somewhat flexible? What are some more-flexible building materials and less-flexible?
- Why is steel commonly used?
- How do you make concrete? Reinforced concrete?

- How do you make iron? Steel? Stainless steel?
- Here is a famous architect who designed skyscrapers.
- Experiment: is reinforced concrete stronger than non-reinforced?

Sr. High Site: How do you design a skyscraper?

- How is a skyscraper anchored so it doesn't fall over in a windstorm?
- Where do you put the windows? Does the glass help hold the building up? What is it for?
- Let's imagine a tall building made of stone blocks like a tall stone wall. What are some problems with this design?
- How are skeleton pieces of tall buildings fastened together, to keep the building flexible? Why does it need to be flexible?
- Describe three skyscrapers with unusual shape.
- Tell the history of the skyscraper.
- Experiment – How do you make a strong, flexible skyscraper?

Week 2 Assignments

Create:

- In a word processor, a headline and paragraphs on your topic. Put your name at the end of the main text in italics, like this: *--Phyllis Wheeler.* Add a list of sources after that. You must use correct grammar and punctuation. Ask an adult to proofread it for you before you transfer it into html. It is much harder to make corrections later.
- A .gif or .jpeg picture that came from you (of appropriate content). (You can save a MicroWorlds picture using this command: ***savehtml "A:\MyNameWebPage***). Or, draw or trace a picture to be scanned. I can also take your picture file home and make it smaller using a photo application we don't have in the lab.
- A folder called *A:\MyName* on a floppy disk. It contains:
- ***page1.gif*** file for the picture and
- ***myname.html*** file for the page itself. You can work on this on any PC—they all have Wordpad. This will contain:
    1. headline and paragraph
    2. a link to the picture

Week 3 Assignment:

From everyone: in your Web page, a link to the home page and two links to appropriate outside pages on your topic. (Find them using www.google.com and keywords from your topic; add the word "kids" to make sure the information isn't too technical.) The text nearby will tell the user that he or she is leaving the Academy of Science server.

From students 1 and 2, cityscape.gif

From student 3, usable pictures from a digital camera, or scanned, of experiment illustrating building principles, plus directions to do experiment.

From students 4, 5, and 6, another illustration for the index page.

Week 4 Assignment:

Everyone's versions of an index page, *index.html*, in a folder called *index*. Exception: student 3 will do a Web page on how to do the experiment. Also, everything else needs to be all wrapped up!

Index page requirements:

1. a folder named *index*, containing an html file named *index*, and image files
2. an appropriate title. Also, a byline--"Creative Home Educators' Co-op"
3. a *cityscape.gif* file, created from our MicroWorlds skyscrapers by Students 1 and 2
4. A list of links calling everyone's individual .html file from the location of the index file.

   For example, the URL link for your individual page will be **../yourname/yourname.html**. The two dots at the front of that are very important, and tell the computer to go up a level in the folder system. The link as the user sees it can describe the content of the page, not the URL. Also, there needs to be a link to the index page on the index page (following Internet convention.) This can say **../index/index.html**.
5. Directions to email questions to someone@somewhere.com

Church or Scouts Web Site

You could make a set of Web pages about a group you belong to, such as scouts or church. These would provide users with information about the group and the people in it.

Week 1:

First we need to gather information. This Web page will tell users about our group. It will be a bit like a news magazine, with interviews of various people and their pictures. Each student will contribute a Web page showing a person who was interviewed, and what he or she said.

For next week, think of someone who helps run the group. Contact that person, in person or on the phone. First, make sure the person hasn't been interviewed already for this project. Ask the person if we may take his or her photo and publish it on the Internet, using only his or her first name. Then ask questions like these: What do you like about this group? What can you tell us about the group? When was it started? What does it do? Whom does it reach?

Write at least eight sentences for junior high, and at least 15 for senior high. Cover your subject thoroughly. Type up the interview. Run the spell check and grammar check. Make corrections. Make sure it is error-free!! Save it on a disk and bring it to class.

If you enjoy photography and would like to take pictures for this project, and you can borrow a digital camera, please let us know as soon as you can.

You can do a page interviewing yourself for extra credit.

Week 2:

Revise interview. Bring in two files you have taken off the Internet that could be used for background, etc.

Week 3:

Complete interview, no errors. Bring in more two files you have taken off the Internet that could be used for background, etc. Start Cool Page file.

Week 4:

Add background, interview text, animation, graphics, sound bytes and links.

Week 5:

Add photo. All work is due.

Appendix II: MicroWorlds Troubleshooting & Procedure Names

Troubleshooting guide

Make sure there are spaces between each word and between word and symbol, for example

colorunder = 15

Make sure each procedure starts with **to** and ends with **end**.

Make sure there are brackets [like these] around lists. List items are separated by spaces. For example,

setsh [horse1 horse2 horse3]

In the above example, note that the names **horse1, horse2** and **horse3** contain no spaces.

For words used as names or nouns (not procedure names, which are actions) make sure there are double-quote marks like these **"word** , made with a single stroke of the double-quote key, or else put the words into a list with brackets. If the error message says "I don't know how to word," then you have forgotten to label **word** as a noun by using either the quote marks or the brackets. So the computer thinks it is an action word. (Or perhaps **word** is a procedure name and you have forgotten to write the procedure for **word**.)

If you can't figure out where the problem is in the program, insert some signal flags. Put lines into the code that say **show "OK** in several places**.** The program will print **OK** in the command center when it passes those spots. Then you will know where to concentrate your efforts, where it is not printing out. Remove these lines when you figure out the problem.

If your program isn't running right, it may be organized poorly. Check the logic of the sequence of things you are calling on the computer to do. If necessary, look at the answers in the answer key.

If you use a built-in procedure name by accident for one of your procedures or variable names, the program won't run right.

If you use a capital O instead of a zero (0), the program won't run right.

If the error message says a procedure needs more inputs, concentrate on the line that calls that procedure and the one following, and look for the proper number of inputs and the proper number of opening and closing brackets.

Built-in Procedures:

cc clear the command center

cg clears graphics

pd puts the current turtle's pen down and requires no inputs and has no outputs

forward or **fd** moves the current turtle in the direction its head is pointing by a number of steps. The number of steps is a required input. (**back** does the opposite)

right turns the current turtle to the right by a number of degrees. The number is a required input. (**left** does the opposite)

wait takes one input, a number.

repeat requires two inputs: a number indicating how many repetitions, and a list of instructions to repeat. A list has brackets [ ] around it.

Presentation Mode: go to the Gadgets menu and click on Presentation Mode. Then click the Start button. To get out of Presentation Mode, click on the black part of the screen outside of MicroWorlds.

talkto "t1, works with turtle named t1

setc setcolor**,** takes a number input, sets the color the turtle is drawing

random takes a number input, randomly produces a number less than the input

setc random 100 will generate a random new color every time it is repeated

fill fills the area the turtle is in with the color the turtle is set to

seth set heading, sets the direction the turtle will move. Takes a number input. 0 is up, is to the right, -90 or 270 is to the left, 180 is down. Example: **seth 90**

setsh, set shape, requires an input which is either a word (must be the name of a shape, such as **setsh "horse1**) or a list of words (must be a list of names of shapes). It changes the shape of the turtle. Point to a particular turtle first using **talkto.** If you give a list of shapes, the program will pick a new shape from the list every time it calls **forward** or **back.**

local reserves and names a storage place

make puts a value in it

show takes one input, a word or a list, and prints it on the Command Center.

: is read, "the value that is in" the storage place or variable

ycor has as output the y coordinate (height on the screen) of the turtle

xcor has as output the x coordinate (distance from the left side) of the turtle

sety takes a number as an input and sets the y coordinate.

setx takes a number as input and sets the x coordinate.

launch has as an input a list of instructions [using brackets like this] to run as a separate process.

Appendix III: HTML Troubleshooting & Commands

Troubleshooting tips:

If your html file doesn't display in your browser, you've forgotten one of the tags or slash marks or made some other tiny error. Enlarge Wordpad/Notepad again make the changes. Carefully go over your file, looking for pairs of tags, one to open and one to close.

The tags should be nested. That is, inside the outer pair of tags of <html> and </html> are some inner pairs, such as <body> and </body>. Between the <body> and </body> tags we might find more tag pairs, such as <p> and </p>. But we can't put a <p> tag before <body> and the corresponding </p> tag after </body>.

When you save your Wordpad/Notepad file, use Save rather than Save As, and type in the .html extension to the file name. You have to click on the type of file to change the way it will save, and save it as a text file. If you are using Notepad, you will probably need to type the .html file extension every time you save. If it saved as name.html.txt, find the file through the My Computer icon, and rename the file by right-clicking on its icon. Get rid of the .txt part.

Commands

To start your page, type this:

> **<html>**
>
> **<head>**
>
> **<title> This title is the one that goes at the very top of the screen. </title>**
>
> **</head>**
>
> **<body>**

Change the background color. Find **<body>.** Change it to:

> **<body bgcolor="#ff0000">.**

Make your headline stand out.

> **<h1> <center> This makes a centered headline in the biggest of font sizes, h1. You can also use h2 , h3, on to h6, the smallest. </h1>**

Some paragraph formats:

<p> This command gives us a new paragraph. </p>

<p> <i> This gives us a new paragraph, in italic. </i> </p>

<p> <b> This gives us a new paragraph, in bold type. </b> </p>

**
 Put this in where you want to start a new line. It's called a line break.**

Don't forget these closing tags:

</body>

</html>

Adding pictures

Put in picture along left side of text:

<p><img src="page1.gif" ALIGN=left> Put lots of text here
</p>

Want to center the image? Don't put it in the same paragraph with the text. Make that

<center> <img src="page1.gif"></center>
<p> Put text here ...</p>

Want an image border of thickness 10 pixels? make that

<center> <img src="page1.gif" border=10></center>

Our image as it comes from MicroWorlds is pretty big. Want it resized? You need to specify the size in pixels. This will take some trial and error, since we don't know how big it is to begin with. The new width and height should be in the same proportion as the old, in order to keep the image looking good. Try this:

<img src="page1.gif" width=300 height=200 >

Let's align it to the right side of the page, and add some horizontal space:

<img src="page1.gif" width=300 height=200 align=right hspace=20>

This will give you an image 300 pixels wide, 200 tall, aligned to the right side of the page, and with 20 pixels of horizontal space added beside the image. (For vertical space, vspace.)

Links

To our own home page:

<a href="../index/index.html"> Go to Homepage </a>

To an outside site:

<a href="http://www.whateverthewebsite.com"> Name of Web Site that shows</a>

To an email address: **<a href=mailto:name@site.com> Click here to e-mail a question</a>**

Bibliography

Allen, Laura, "Cityscapes in Logo," published on the Logo Foundation web site (http://el.media.mit.edu/logo-foundation/pubs/papers/cityscapes.html), copyright 1993.

Castro, Elizabeth, *HTML for the World Wide Web, Fifth edition, with XHTML and CSS: Visual Quickstart Guide*, Peachpit Press, Berkeley, Calif., 2003.

Yoder, Sharon, *MicroWorlds 2.0: Hypermedia Project Development & Logo Scripting*, International Society for Technology in Education, Eugene, Oregon, 1997

Answers

Note: Many answers are contained in the text. This key contains those that are not in the text.

#5 answers

```
to square
   ; draws a square of 50 units
   forward 50 right 90 wait 1
   forward 50 right 90 wait 1
   forward 50 right 90 wait 1
   forward 50 right 90 wait 1
end
```

becomes

```
to square
   ;draws a square of 50 units
   repeat 4 [forward 50 right 90 wait 1]
end
```

Drawing a starburst

```
to starburst
   repeat 360 [right 1 forward 50 back  50]
end
```

Drawing a triangle

```
to triangle
   ; draws a triangle of 3 sides of 50
   repeat 3 [forward 50 right 120 wait 1]
end


to climb.to.roof
   ; takes turtle to position to draw roof
   pu
   seth 0
   forward 50
   right 30
   pd
end


to Main
   ; draws a simple house
   cg
   pd
   square
   climb.to.roof
   triangle
end
```

#6 answers (procedures in alphabetical order)

```
================
to Main
   ;draws a house
   cg
   pd
   square
   climb.to.roof
   triangle
   move.to.door
   door
   move.to.window
   window
   colorhouse
end
==================

to climb.to.roof
   ; takes turtle to position to draw roof
   pu
   seth 0
   forward 50
   right 30
   pd
end

to colorhouse
   pu
   seth -90
   forward 5
   setc 15
   fill
end

to door
   pd
   repeat 2 [forward 20 right 90 forward 10 right 90  wait 1]
end

to move.to.door
   pu
   seth 180
   forward 50
   left 90
   forward 20
   seth 0
end


to move.to.window
   pu
   seth 90
   forward 13
   left 90
   forward 30
end

to square
   ;draws a square of 50 units
   repeat 4 [forward 50 right 90 wait 1]
end

to triangle
   ; draws a triangle of 3 sides of 50
   repeat 3 [forward 50 right 120 wait 1]
end

to window
   pd
   repeat 4 [forward 15 right 90]
end
```

#16 answers

```
to Main
   cc
   testSize
end

to testSize
   local "size
   make "size 5
   local "height
   make "height 60
   show :size
   show :height
   make "size sum :size 3
   show :size
end
```

#17 answers

```
to window :size
   repeat 2 [forward 15 * :size  right 90 forward 20 * :size
right 90]
end
```

```
-------------------------------
to Main :housesize
    ;draws a house
    cg
    pd
    square :housesize
    climb.to.roof :housesize
    triangle :housesize
     door :housesize
end

to climb.to.roof :height
    ; takes turtle to position to draw roof
    pu
    forward 50 * :height
    right 30
    pd
end

to door :doorsize
    pu
    seth 180
    pd
    forward 50 * :doorsize
   left 90
   forward 15 * :doorsize
   pd
   repeat 4 [forward 20 * :doorsize left 90 wait 1]
end

to square :length
   ;draws a square of 50 units
    repeat 4 [forward 50 * :length right 90 wait 1]
end

to triangle :trisize
   ; draws a triangle
   repeat 3 [forward 50 * :trisize right 120 wait 1]
end
```

#18 suggested answers

Bee with wobble down

```
=========================
to Main
   cg
   cc
   talkto "t1
   setsh [bee1 bee2]
   seth 90
   repeat 200 [fly 1 10 wobble 10]
end
==========================

to wobble :howFar
   local "originalHeading
   make "originalHeading heading
   seth 180
   forward :howFar
   wait 1
   back :howFar
   seth :originalHeading
end

to start
   main
end

to fly :stepsize :qsteps
   repeat :qsteps
   [forward :stepsize wait 1]
end
```

Extra credit: bee wobbles up and down

```
=========================
to Main
   cg
   cc
   talkto "t1
   setsh [bee1 bee2]
   seth 90
   repeat 200 [fly 10 10  upwobble 10 fly 10 10 d_wobble 10]
end
==========================

to d_wobble :howFar
   local "originalHeading
   make "originalHeading heading
   seth 180
   forward :howFar
   wait 1
   back :howFar
   seth :originalHeading
end
```

```
to fly :stepsize :qsteps
   repeat :qsteps
   [forward :stepsize wait 1]
end

to start
   main
end

to upwobble :howFar
   local "originalHeading
   make "originalHeading heading
   seth 0
   forward :howFar
   wait 1
   back :howFar
   seth :originalHeading
end
```

#19 suggested answers

Exercise 1
Make a "Hop" button.

```
====================
to Main
   cc
   talkto "t1
   setsh [dog1 dog2]
   seth 270
      repeat 200
            [Walk 10 10]
   end
=====================

to doHop :width
   local "originalX
   make "originalX xcor
   setx sum xcor :width
    wait 1
   setx :originalX
end

to doJump :height
   local "originalY
   make "originalY ycor
   sety sum ycor :height
   wait 1
   sety :originalY
end

to hop
   doHop 45  ;(change this number to several
other          ;numbers and see the result)
end

 to jump
   doJump 40
end

to Start
   Main
end

to walk :stepsize :qsteps
   repeat :qsteps
      [forward :stepsize  wait 1]
end
```

Exercise 2

Change Main as follows:

```
to Main
   cc
   talkto "t1
   setsh [horse1 horse2 horse3]
   seth 90
   repeat 200
            [Walk 10 10]
  end
```

Exercise 3

Change Main as follows:

```
   repeat 200
            [Walk 2 8]
```

Exercise 4

Change walk as follows:

```
to walk :stepsize :qsteps
   repeat :qsteps
     [setx sum xcor :stepsize
      wait 1 ]
end
```

(Note: without forward, the animal doesn't appear to walk any more.)

#20 suggested answers

ex. 1 & 2 Add two turtles; program the color cyan to respond to colorCyanHit. Spray some cyan paint near the castle.

```
================
to Main
   cc
   talkto "t2
   setsh [dog1 dog2]
   seth 270
   launch
     [
     repeat 200
        [Walk 10 10]
     ]
   talkto "t3
   setsh [skater1 skater2 skater3]
   seth 90
   launch
     [
     repeat 200
        [walk 10 10]
     ]
   talkto "t5
   setsh [tornado1 tornado2]
   seth 90
    launch
    [
    repeat 200
            [walk 10 10]
     ]
end
====================

 to colorCyanHit
    doJump 80 200
    poof
    wait 5
    unpoof
end
```

```
to colorGrayHit
   doJump 50 100
end

to doJump :height :distance
   local "originalY
   make "originalY ycor
   sety sum ycor :height
   wait 1
   forward :distance
   wait 1
   sety :originalY
end

to jump
   doJump 30 30
end
to poof
   talkto "t4
    setsh "cloud
end

to Start
   Main
end
```

```
to unpoof
   talkto "t4
   setsh random 12
end

to walk :stepsize :qsteps
   repeat :qsteps
      [forward :stepsize
      wait 1]
end
```

ex. 3

Draw a spiral maze using the drawing center and a thick gray line. Program the color gray to respond to colorGrayHit. Here is one possibility for a maze, not the best—can you do a better one?

```
==========================
to Main
   cc
   talkto "t1
     repeat 2000 [ forward 1 ]
end
===========================
to colorGrayHit
    back 3 wait 1
    right random 270
    wait 1
    forward 3 wait 1
end


to Start
   Main
end
```

Index